If there is one constant in American history, it is that *assaults against us forge unity,* and that senseless violence will

ShootingStraight

inspire us to search for deeper meanings. The Second Amendment not only expresses our right to keep and bear arms, it also makes it clear that *public security is* ▶▶▶

(continued on page 2)

ShootingStraight

TELLING THE
TRUTH ABOUT GUNS
IN AMERICA

Wayne LaPierre and
James Jay Baker

Since 1947
REGNERY
PUBLISHING, INC.
An Eagle Publishing Company • Washington, DC

Library of Congress Cataloging-in-Publication Data

LaPierre, Wayne R., 1949-
  Shooting straight : telling the truth about guns in America / Wayne LaPierre and James Jay Baker.
      p. cm.
Includes bibliographical references and index.
  ISBN 0-89526-123-5
  1. Gun control—United States. 2. Firearms ownership—United States.
3. Firearms—Law and legislation—United States. I. Baker, James Jay.
II. Title.
  HV7436 .L3654 2002
  323.4'3—dc21

                            2002010081

Published in the United States by
Regnery Publishing, Inc.
An Eagle Publishing Company
One Massachusetts Avenue, NW
Washington, DC 20001

Visit us at www.regnery.com

Distributed to the trade by
National Book Network
4720-A Boston Way
Lanham, MD 20706

Printed on acid-free paper
Manufactured in the United States of America

10 9 8 7 6 5 4 3 2 1

Books are available in quantity for promotional or premium use. Write to Director of Special Sales, Regnery Publishing, Inc., One Massachusetts Avenue, NW, Washington, DC 20001, for information on discounts and terms or call (202) 216-0600.

For all the activists across America
who have dedicated themselves
to preserving the Second Amendment
for future generations

Contents

Introduction **by Charlton Heston** ix

• • •

Chapter One **Piggybacking on Terror** 1

• • •

Chapter Two **Your Handbook on Gun Issues** 21

• • •

Chapter Three **Citizen Rights** 59

• • •

Chapter Four **(Real) Homeland Defense** 81

• • •

Chapter Five **Gun Safety** 93

• • •

Chapter Six **Second Amendment Follies** 105

• • •

Chapter Seven **The Gun-Control Hive** 121

• • •

Chapter Eight **The Litigation Machine** 131

• • •

Chapter Nine **Hollywood and Guns** 139

• • •

Chapter Ten **Little Acorns and Bad Treaties** 149

• • •

Chapter Eleven **Gun Control and "Silver Bullets"** 161

• • •

Conclusion 173

• • •

Postscript 179

• • •

Appendix Zell Miller's "Picket Line of Freedom" 183

• • •

Notes 191

• • •

Acknowledgments 203

• • •

Index 205

Introduction

Ican't think of two people more qualified to write the definitive book on the struggle to protect the Second Amendment than my good friends Wayne LaPierre and James Jay Baker. With nearly half a century of experience between them, Wayne and Jim have lived and breathed the right to keep and bear arms for the better part of their adult lives, and are among the most recognizable and respected voices for firearms freedom in America today.

In *Shooting Straight*, Wayne and Jim lay waste to the most common myths about guns and gun ownership in America, and offer a thoroughly convincing argument that the individual right to bear arms is as relevant now as it was at the founding of our republic. In light of recent events, the message about personal freedom and individual responsibility they bring us in this comprehensive book is especially welcome.

—Charlton Heston

Chapter One

Piggybacking on Terror

The Sly New Push to Ban Firearms

Deena Burnett on phone to husband, United Flight 93 hijack victim:
My God. They seem to be taking planes and driving them into designated landmarks all over the East Coast. It's as if hell has been unleashed.

Passenger Tom Burnett to wife Deena:...We're going to do something....We can't wait. Deena, if they are going to run this plane into the ground, we're going to do something.

Passenger Todd Beamer (overheard by GTE operator): Are you guys ready? Let's roll.

America is fighting back.
Many around the world seem surprised. They shouldn't be.

Throughout history, fanatics and despots have assumed that we Americans were too soft, too wrapped in our creature comforts, to bother to retaliate against violence against our citizens. And throughout history, these same fanatics and despots have been taught a lesson. They've learned the true American character before being consigned to what President Bush aptly describes as "history's unmarked grave of discarded lies."

This American spirit of resistance to tyranny showed itself on the very morning of September 11, when passengers on United Flight 93 put down their cell phones, rose from their seats, grabbed whatever weapons were at hand, and prevented the hijackers from destroying the White House, the U.S. Capitol, or what was left of the Pentagon.

Only months later, when the armed forces of the United States executed the liberation of Afghanistan, we also liberated ourselves from the elitist attitude that has long disparaged the use of force in the defense of freedom.

An awakening is taking place. And the stark, unpolitically correct truth is, Americans are feeling pretty good about fighting back. Pollster Richard Wirthlin found that prior to September 11, Americans who felt that the country was on the wrong track constituted a growing majority. And what was their reaction, once the planes had dived and the towers had crumbled? Wirthlin found that the balance had precisely flip-flopped in favor of the "right direction."

How can this be?

If there is one constant in American history, it is that assaults against us forge unity, and senseless violence inspires us to seek deeper meanings. Americans are reconnecting with the Founders' vision for America—of a nation of free citizens, armed and prepared to preserve their liberties. To make sure that we would have the means to secure our freedoms, the Founders enshrined their vision in the Second Amendment. The Second Amendment was far from an afterthought. The Founders understood that it would be, as NRA president Charlton Heston puts it, "the eternal bodyguard" of our other liberties. This amendment not only expresses our right as citizens to keep and bear arms, it also makes it clear that *public security is the public's business.*

Only by being armed and prepared, the Founders understood, would we as a people best be able to preserve our liberties against all forms of tyranny, foreign and domestic.

Tyrants are not just foreign dictators, but any enemy who tries to rule our lives through fear. We know the names and faces of our foreign enemies. Who are our domestic enemies? For the most part, the main domestic threat to a law-abiding American man or woman is likely to be a fellow citizen who has decided to become a predator. The likeliest danger we face is from a mugger, a home-invasion robber, a rapist, and sometimes a midnight abductor or a serial killer.

[The Constitution preserves] the advantage of being armed which Americans possess over the people of almost every other nation... [where] the governments are afraid to trust the people with arms.

—James Madison, The Federalist, *No. 46*

Changes in the way we respond to this threat reflect a similar kind of awakening of the American spirit. The seeds of that awakening are present in a thought-provoking 1993 essay by scholar Jeffrey R. Snyder, who criticized the advice police and media often give to victims—that the safest and best way to deal with a criminal is to put up no resistance. Snyder wrote:

> For years, feminists have labored to educate people that rape is not about sex, but about domination, degradation, and control. Evidently, someone needs to inform the law enforcement establishment and the media that kidnapping, robbery, carjacking, and assault are not about property.
> Crime is not only a complete disavowal of the social contract, but also a commandeering of the victim's person and liberty. If the individual's dignity lies in the fact that he is a moral agent engaging in actions of his own will, in free exchange with others, then crime always violates the victim's dignity. It is, in fact, an act of enslavement. Your wallet, your purse, or your car may not be worth your life, but your dignity is; and if it is not worth fighting for, it can hardly be said to exist.[1]

President Bush, in the context of terrorism, has correctly cast the debate in moral terms. In this same way, Snyder identified what was so wrong, so *evil*, about crime. It possesses the power to dehumanize good people. It is, in fact, just a pedestrian form of terrorism.

For most Americans, the odds of suffering such an attack at the hands of a criminal are many times greater than the odds of being attacked by a terrorist. Are we willing to meet these domestic threats as courageously as our servicemen are meeting terrorist threats from abroad?

Long before September 11, Jeffrey Snyder wondered the same thing.

"Crime is rampant because the law-abiding, each of us, condone it, excuse it, permit it, submit to it," he wrote. "We permit and encourage it because we do not fight back, immediately, then and there, where it happens. Crime is not rampant because we do not have enough prisons, because judges and prosecutions are too soft, because the police are hamstrung with absurd technicalities. The defect is there, in our character. We are a nation of cowards and shirkers."

That is a deliberate overstatement. Recent history has shown us to be anything but a nation of cowards. But that one provocative statement posed a harsh but useful question for Americans at a critical time in our history. For decades, violent crimes like murder and rape, as well as serious property crimes, had steadily risen—most of all in big urban centers where guns were outlawed or so restricted that they provided no credible deterrent to crime. Law-abiding citizens could recount for you, almost as a matter of pride, how many muggings they had endured. Parking garages became gauntlets for women to enter and exit as fast as possible, all the time fearing being carjacked or worse. Public streets in some parts of America came to resemble a war zone.

For a long time, unfortunately, we Americans responded to crime with passivity. We yearned to set aside safe zones, to carve out a block, or a school, or a part of town, and say, "Not here." And yet we learned that when we designate safe zones, we permit, by implication, areas where criminal behavior is tolerated, even expected. And we learned that passivity in the face of evil makes us unwitting accomplices in our own destruction.

Why did we let this happen to our country? The crime wave that built in the 1960s and swept over America into the 1990s was not a big, explosive event like a terrorist attack. It rose slowly, steadily, and we—like the proverbial frog in the gradually boiling pot—had become too reconciled, too comfortable, with living in the midst of crime. We were in danger of becoming what Snyder feared—a nation of moral cowards.

Then something happened that, in its own slow, quiet way, was as remarkable and as awesome as the American response to terrorism. As a people, we began to take back our homes, our streets, our cities. Here, too, the American spirit of resistance is on display.

We fought back by electing mayors who weren't afraid to let our police enforce the law (including on petty crimes like vandalism, which, if left unpunished, encourage more serious crimes). We got tougher about sentencing criminals. And, most of all, we turned the tables on crime by returning to the vision of the Founders and exercising our Second Amendment rights.

Fifteen years ago, a law-abiding citizen could legally carry a concealed weapon in only ten states. Now thirty-three states, with more than half of the U.S. population, have passed laws mandating that authorities "shall issue" right-to-carry permits that allow millions of citizens to keep guns in their cars, under their coats, or in their purses. America has more gun owners than ever. What has been the result?

Gun ownership is now at an all-time high. And violent crime, by the year 2000, hit a twenty-two-year low.

The nation's violent crime rate has declined every year since 1991. Murder is at a thirty-five-year low. Total violent crime has decreased by almost one-third. With more women than ever carrying guns, rape has decreased by 24.2 percent. Robbery has decreased by almost 50 percent.

To be fair, a host of factors are responsible for this decrease in crime, not just the widespread increase in gun ownership. Thanks to NRA-supported measures, in many jurisdictions criminals who use guns to commit crimes are being put away in federal prison. Social and demographic factors played a major role.

Still, only the most hidebound proponent of "gun control" could fail to notice that some of the most dramatic decreases in crime are taking place in states where citizens are exercising their Second Amendment rights under a right-to-carry law.

Laws that forbid the carrying of arms... disarm only those who are neither inclined nor determined to commit crimes.... Such laws make things worse for the assaulted and better for the assailants; they serve rather to encourage than to prevent homicides, for an unarmed man may be attacked with greater confidence than an armed man.

—Thomas Jefferson's "Commonplace Book," 1774–1776, quoting from On Crimes and Punishment, *by criminologist Cesare Beccaria, 1764*

No free man shall ever be debarred the use of arms.

—Jefferson, Proposed Virginia Constitution, 1776

In 2000, states with right-to-carry laws had lower violent crime rates on average, compared to the rest of the country. If you are lucky enough to live in one of these states, your risk of being murdered is 28.4 percent lower than the national average; of being robbed, 37.7 percent lower; and of being assaulted, 16.5 percent lower. The only states that experienced increases in their murder rates between 1991 (the year national crime levels began to decrease) and 2000 were three states *without* right-to-carry laws (Rhode Island, Nebraska, and Kansas).[2]

What role did gun control play in reducing crime? Gun control is absent from the FBI's list of reasons why crime decreased in the 1990s. People who love the Brady Act will tell you that this gun-control law (which established a waiting period and background check on handgun purchases) was responsible, as well as a new federal ban on "assault weapons." A little scrutiny shows these claims to be ridiculous.

First of all, the Brady Act and "assault weapons" law did not go into effect until 1994—three years after violent crime began its national decrease. Even sympathetic researchers[3] found that the

Brady Act had no effect on homicide and suicide rates. A National Institute of Justice study mandated by Congress determined that the "assault weapons" law had no effect on crime because these firearms (which, despite this stigmatizing label, are simply self-loading, semi-automatic weapons) were *never used by criminals in the first place.*[4] And in any event, the law does not forbid semi-automatic firearms. It merely requires that certain cosmetic attachments be left off—a distinction that would not keep them from being used in a crime, if someone were inclined to do so. In fact, the number of these rifles (made before and after this law) is greater than ever.

So how to account for the role guns play in the decrease of crime?

The best answers can be found not in statistics, but in stories that you hear in every community, stories of self-defense often ignored or rejected outright by the mainstream media.

Consider what happened at the Appalachian School of Law in rural Grundy, Virginia, on January 16, 2002. On that day, one Peter Odighizuwa, a forty-three-year-old man and sometime student, went on a shooting rampage. If you remember the media reports, you'll recall that he used a .380-caliber pistol to shoot and kill the school's dean and two others before students "subdued" him.

Predictably, the shooting prompted an outcry to restrict the people's right to bear arms. What was most important about the murders in Grundy, however, was the part that went virtually unreported: Two of the students who confronted Odighizuwa and subdued him were themselves armed. The quick reaction of two students—Mikael Gross and Tracy Bridges—saved multiple lives.

John R. Lott, Jr., a noted scholar of crime and gun laws whose discoveries will be critical to our argument in the pages ahead, wrote:

> Mikael was outside the law school just returning from lunch when Peter Odighizuwa started his attack. Tracy was in a classroom waiting for class to start. When the shots rang out, utter chaos erupted. "People were running everywhere," Mikael said. "They were jumping behind cars, running out in front of traffic, trying to get away."

Mikael and Tracy did something quite different: Both immediately ran to their cars and got their guns. Along with Ted
Besen (who was unarmed), the two men approached Odighizuwa from different sides. As Tracy explained it, "I aimed my
gun at him, and Peter tossed his gun down. Ted approached
Peter, and Peter hit Ted in the jaw. Ted pushed him back and
we all jumped on."[5]

If you remember the story, this part of the event may still come to
you as news. Why? Lott found that out of 280 separate news stories
in the week after the shootings, just *four* stories bothered to mention
that the students who stopped the attack had guns.

The *Washington Post*'s coverage was typical. The heroes had simply "helped subdue" the killer. Many stories wrote about the gunman being "tackled." The big, urban media are just too wedded to
"gun control" to bother with the facts. Only the *Richmond Times-
Dispatch* and the *Charlotte Observer* mentioned that armed students
confronted the attacker.

We can all take pride in the dramatic decreases in crime. But we
must keep in mind that these reductions in crime, as large as they
are, are dwarfed by the total magnitude of crime in America. The
truth is, the reductions of the 1990s are much like shaving off the top
third of a mountain. But the mountain is still there. *The bulk of the
increase in violent crime rates in America over the last hundred years is still
with us.*

So if you reduce all the social science about crime and guns in
America, it comes down to two "headlines" (the first of which, by the
way, you would never see on the front page of nearly any major daily
newspaper in America).

That first headline could read, *Widespread Gun Ownership Brings
Down Crime Rate.*

The second could read, *Crime Rate Down, But Overall Levels Still
High.*

There are still more than 500 violent offenses for every 100,000
citizens, or about 1.4 million violent crimes committed against

Americans. This number includes more than 15,500 Americans murdered, almost 100,000 forcible rapes reported, almost 1 million aggravated assaults.[6]

Overall, from 1960 to 1998, total U.S. crime increased by 344 percent, violent crime by 307 percent, and property crime by 350 percent.[7]

The astonishing fact is that these numbers would be higher—immensely higher—without widespread gun ownership. Criminologists Gary Kleck and Marc Gertz found that "robbery and assault victims who used a gun to resist were less likely to be attacked or to suffer an injury than those who used any other method of self-protection or those who did not resist at all."[8]

When they analyzed the numbers, they found that firearms are used for self-protection an astonishing 2.5 million times a year.

Most of the time, these firearms are not fired, and sometimes need not even be brandished, to prevent these crimes. In 1995, a criminologist who was a strong proponent of gun control reviewed these findings. He declared, "I do not like their [the criminologists'] conclusions that having a gun can be useful, but I cannot fault their methodology. They have tried earnestly to meet all objections in advance and have done exceedingly well."[9]

An earlier study found that 34 percent of felons had been "scared off, shot at, wounded or captured by an armed victim," and that 40 percent of felons have not committed crimes, fearing potential victims were armed.[10]

That's a lot of crime prevented.

A lot of women spared the ordeal of rape.

A lot of potential murder victims walking around alive and safe.

These are the facts. And these facts are decidedly inconvenient for a gun-control lobby that has grown in wealth and sophistication throughout the 1990s. Think about it. Put yourself in the position of a gun-control advocate. What can you say? Where can you go in the face of such overwhelming evidence against your position?

There is, of course, only one place to go when the facts are against you.

To stay in the debate, you must twist the facts. You must exploit tragedy. You must engage in demagoguery.

• • •

Smoke was still curling over the ruins of the World Trade Center when the gun-control lobby swung into action, seizing on that tragedy to score points in the political arena.

Seven days after the attack, the Brady Center to Prevent Gun Violence issued its first press release linking terrorism and the danger of guns in the home. About three months after the attack, the Brady Center issued a report, "Guns and Terror: How Terrorists Exploit Our Weak Gun Laws." Despite the fact that all nineteen terrorists commandeered airplanes not with guns, but with boxcutters and other crude knives, the cover of the report was adorned with an evil-looking man in a typical Moslem outfit peering at the reader through the scope of a rifle. The report should have been named: "How the Gun-Control Lobby Exploits Tragedy to Terrorize Americans."[11]

Less than a month after September 11, gun-control advocates at the Violence Policy Center chimed in, issuing a report called "Voting from the Rooftops: How the Gun Industry Armed Osama bin Laden, Other Foreign and Domestic Terrorists and Common Criminals with .50-Caliber Sniper Rifles."

After reading that, you might want to throw this book down, lock the door, and close the shutters (after looking up and down the street for a terrorist). What's this about? The Violence Policy Center is harping on the sale, *in the late 1980s,* of twenty-five high-powered, military-style sniper rifles that were provided to the Afghan resistance of the Soviet invasion *by action of the U.S. government.* You'll recall that during the Reagan administration, there was strong bipartisan support in Washington, D.C., for people who, at that time, were popularly known as "Afghan freedom-fighters." Yes, some of them later became terrorists and turned against the United States. That's hardly a news flash. Yet the Violence Policy Center treats this chapter of U.S. foreign policy as if it were a domestic gun issue.[12]

Do you think that's an honest treatment of the issue? Do you think that's a very respectful way to deal with the memory of September 11?

Chris W. Cox, the new executive director of the NRA's Institute for Legislative Action, is a hunting buddy of the authors, and the point man for making our case on campaign finance reform and other critical issues. Many people who represent issues on Capitol Hill speak in a roundabout way. Chris doesn't mince words when it comes to the red herring of terrorism and gun shows.

"This lowers the level of debate," he says. "September 11 had nothing to do with lawful gun owners and lawful gun shows. This should be offensive to every American and every gun owner."

You might think that at least elected officials would be above exploiting tragedy in this way for political gain. You would be wrong.

Before 2001 was out, Senators Ted Kennedy and Chuck Schumer pushed a bill that would amount to national gun-buyer registration. They have long wanted the Department of Justice to retain the records of the National Instant Check System (NICS), the computerized system that exists solely to determine whether a person seeking to buy a gun has a criminal record. By retaining the records of the law-abiding citizens who clear the system, the Department of Justice would in effect create a national database with which to confiscate guns. (As you'll see in the next chapter, that is not as far-fetched as it sounds. The recent history of other countries, including Canada, shows how registration quickly leads to confiscation.)

How did Kennedy and Schumer exploit September 11?

Their bill is now called the "Use NICS in Terrorism Investigations Act." But it's still the same old gun-control bill.

"Now we've got the terrorist issue," boasts Representative John Conyers of Michigan, in talking about his innocuous-sounding proposal for extending background checks that would effectively kill gun shows in America. "There are very few in the general population who are going to tolerate a loophole through which these weapons are allowed into the war to support terrorism. That is a no-brainer at this point."[13]

All of these efforts pale in comparison to the sleek, sophisticated antigun campaign that goes by the winsome name of Americans for Gun Safety (AGS). On December 14, 2001, they put out a statement on the conviction of a Lebanese man named Ali Boumelhem for weapons charges.

The AGS statement drips with ominous speculation of a sort one used to read on the backs of dime-store novels.

It reads: "We don't know whether the Boumelhem case is part of a pattern or an isolated lone wolf. But we do know this—the agents of terror operating on our soil have navigated our freedoms to exploit airports, flight schools, colleges, financial institutions and libraries to strike at the heart of our country. Maybe they are not interested in using guns as part of their terror plans. Maybe they are interested only in dramatic attacks like bombs, planes, and the like. But the notion that they have not—or cannot—figure out that they can buy guns at gun shows with no questions asked is no longer credible."

The truth is, there are no laws or background checks that will keep a determined, sophisticated terrorist from getting his hands on a gun anywhere in the world, if that is what he wants to do. If the AGS reports are to be believed, this beloved American institution of gun shows—as old as the Republic, one cherished as much by gun collectors as auto buffs love auto shows, or devotees of earthenware love porcelain shows—has become a squalid bazaar of eye-patched, scar-faced international arms merchants who would scare the pants off Indiana Jones.

The AGS freely throws around charges about terrorist organizations like Hamas and Hezbollah flocking to American gun shows— but the real target is the ordinary, law-abiding American who wants to sell his or her late father's deer rifle.

We won't get into a point-by-point refutation of these charges here. We'll save that and discussion of the so-called "gun-show loophole" for the next chapter. The point is that after losing on so many fronts, the antigun crowd is back in business, fueled by rumor-mongering and appeals to fear.

What makes AGS insidious is that it has explicitly broken with other antigun groups in accepting the constitutionality of gun ownership. Its Web site offers a sepia-toned, nostalgic picture of a hunter toting a shotgun. It strikes a reasonable pose, suggesting that it doesn't want to get rid of guns, just make sure that they are used safely.

What is going on here? The people behind AGS understand that they have lost time and again on efforts to move toward explicit, direct banning of the use of guns for personal safety. So they are seeking to enact laws that would make it harder for law-abiding people to own guns. They are doing this one waiting period, one restriction at a time. These are people who know when to give up on a frontal assault and try to flank the enemy.

What is AGS?

The most public faces of AGS are those of Senators John McCain and Joseph Lieberman.

It was McCain, you'll recall, who, backed by friendly big media, goaded his fellow senators until he passed what the media uncritically call campaign finance reform. Under this law, big media conglomerates like Viacom, the Disney Corporation, and General Electric have unlimited rights to spend money talking about issues and candidates (which, of course, is their constitutional right). These big, wealthy institutions own broadcasting companies and spend millions lobbying Congress, yet campaign finance reform leaves them alone. Left out in the cold are ordinary citizens and advocacy groups ranging from the National Rifle Association (NRA) to the American Civil Liberties Union, who would be forbidden by law from expressing their views in the weeks before an election. Under this new law, the NRA isn't even allowed to respond to charges by the broadcast media for weeks before an election. The punishment for violating this complicated law is prison sentences and stiff fines.

The intent of such a law is obvious. It is aimed at stifling the voices of gun-owning American citizens.

In referring to this measure, ultraliberal senator Paul Wellstone mentioned the NRA, and then complained: "More than 70 percent of these sham electioneering ads sponsored by groups are attack ads that denigrate a candidate's image or character as opposed to 2 percent, the good news, of the candidate-sponsored ads."

Did you get that? Any ad critical of a federal candidate is a sham and therefore worthy of official censorship. Any ad run by the candidate himself is, by definition, "the good news."

Wellstone went on to complain about advocacy organizations like the NRA, "These groups are accountable to virtually no one, to nobody....Any group, any organization, any individual can finance any kind of ad they want."[14]

Imagine that! Free speech in America.

The only good news is that many of these gag orders imposed by the campaign finance "reform" measure are flatly unconstitutional. In April 2002, the NRA and its four million members were the first to file a lawsuit against this unconstitutional infringement of our ability to use the First Amendment rights to defend our Second Amendment rights.

But the senatorial jihad against the NRA continues in the guise of "gun safety." AGS spent a quarter of a million dollars promoting John McCain in film commercials that ran in theaters in forty-four states (that must have been one of those 2 percent of ads that Paul Wellstone certifies as a "good ad").

Now that the campaign finance law is in place, millions will be spent to help McCain and Lieberman push for antigun legislation through Capitol Hill by linking terrorism to gun shows.

This is an ambitious effort. Where is the money for this coming from?

The spectrum of antigun groups are funded by foundations that in turn are financed by some of the largest corporations in America, from IBM to Sara Lee. Senator McCain, so disdainful of "special interest" money, is attaching his star to AGS, which is funded by the deep pockets of a billionaire named Andrew McKelvey. Now in his mid-sixties, McKelvey tools around on a 110-foot yacht and a jet once owned by golf great Greg Norman. While you may not know of him, you probably know of one of his most successful ventures, the job-placement Web site Monster.com.[15] McKelvey is no friend of the gun owner. A former board member of Handgun Control, McKelvey famously complained, "I'm sick to death of the NRA."

Before bankrolling AGS, McKelvey backed a flurry of municipal lawsuits aimed at bankrupting the firearms industry.[16]

When McCain's campaign bill was at a critical juncture in 2001, McKelvey ponied up more than $125,000 to finance a blitz of television ads urging citizens to demand passage of McCain's bill—further demonstration that the relationship between McCain and McKelvey is like that of a shark and a pilot fish. (Again, those television ads must have been Wellstone's "good" ones.)[17]

An AGS memo, leaked to the public, reveals the real intentions of this group and its use of centrist language. Penn, Schoen & Berland, longtime consultants to Bill Clinton and Al Gore, advised the group: "The term 'gun control' should be dropped and replaced with 'gun safety,' 'responsible gun use,' or 'accountability in gun use.'" In other words, slap a fresh new slogan over the same old gun control. An internal memo, also leaked to the public, reveals that AGS's "top national priority" is "passage of licensing and/or registration in the next Congress."[18]

An AGS guideline for members' advocacy is taken directly from a UN primer on garnering global support to spend your tax dollars on Third World AIDS victims. The instructions for "Applied Media Advocacy Skills" were prepared at the University of California at Berkeley, long a hothouse for nurturing the loony left. Among other tactics, the Berkeley manual details how to cultivate the news media, "using anniversaries to make news on guns," based around such ghoulish tactics as keying events such as political assassinations, celebrity murders, schoolyard shootings, and even a Fourth of July holiday observance on the theme "Independence from fear of violence." (How the Founders would spin in their graves over that one.)[19]

The staffing of AGS, despite its centrist appeal, also reveals that it is the same old antigun crowd we know so well. Heading the new group is Jonathan Cowan, formerly chief of staff for one of the most liberal members of the Clinton cabinet, HUD Secretary Andrew Cuomo. Cuomo appointed himself "gun-control czar" of the Clinton-Gore administration and proudly announced his agenda for fighting crime in public housing: threatening thousands of foolish and non-sensical lawsuits against gunmakers.

Still, AGS has enough money to present any image it wants. And the image it presents, one of bland moderation, allowed it to spend nearly $3 million in Colorado and Oregon, where it supported anti-gun ballot initiatives in 2000. The campaign succeeded, but AGS's tactics were revealing. It demonized gun shows, hoodwinking moderate and reasonable voters into taking us all one step closer to gun registration and eventual confiscation.

It is easy to see where AGS is going. The group hopes to recruit the so-called soccer moms who loomed so large in electing Clinton and Gore to power. According to another leaked report, political consultants advised AGS to make "suburban women...[the] primary target" because they are "already convinced" of the AGS agenda and are easier to "convert to activists." Suburban men are identified as a "secondary target," whom recruiters were warned to "not antagonize; respect the needs of legitimate gun owners."

In short, consultants are telling them to scare women. They should know that there are plenty of "soccer moms" who are gun owners and NRA members. Women are smart enough to know that the real threat comes from drug dealers, carjackers, and violent felons.

Among the "compelling strategies" to emerge from an AGS study was "gun owner safety education...supported by all, even NRA members." But on the issue of teaching gun safety to kids, although the report identifies the idea as a compelling strategy, it notes that AGS is "opposed."

Hard to believe, isn't it? That a group whose very name is gun safety would be opposed to teaching firearm safety? All they offer is a paltry "dos and don'ts" list of advice on gun safety on their Web site. To obtain gun-safety instruction for yourself or your children, you would have to go to a gun owners' association. You would probably go to the NRA, which has spent more than $20 million in recent years to work with local school districts and police units around America to teach gun safety to thirteen million children. In its very name is the core of deception: "Americans for Gun Safety" has zero members and no gun-safety programs.

Those children are, literally, America's and the NRA's future. Because the truth is, in the years to come, we may need to be armed as never before. As the government necessarily retargets some of its investigative and law-enforcement resources away from crime and toward terrorism, the thin blue line will be all that much thinner for the law-abiding American. We will see fewer FBI agents concerned with crime, and more state and local police whose time will be taken up with terrorist-related exercises and homeland defense.

In staking out their positions, the gun controllers make their intent obvious. They wish to marginalize gun owners by painting us as extremists. They trade in making reasonable-sounding claims, in order to make the NRA reactionary.

After all, how could anyone be against a "cooling off" period before buying a gun? What kind of Neanderthal would support "cop-killer" bullets? Or be in favor of "plastic guns" that terrorists can smuggle onto airplanes? Or oppose restrictions on "assault rifles"?

Again and again, the gun-control lobby, backed by friendly media, invents issues and plays word games to make gun owners appear unreasonable, unyielding, stuck in a frontier past.

The truth is, in recent years the NRA has bent over backwards to support real gun-safety legislation. And the previous Clinton administration, unwilling to give up on its agenda of gun control, killed these measures. They would not compromise.

Don't be surprised. Gun safety is not their agenda. Gun control is.

The NRA supports legislation to require the mandatory issuance of safety locks with the sale of every gun. (The NRA opposes, however, making the use of safety locks mandatory.)

The NRA supports tough laws to keep violent juveniles from ever legally buying a gun.

These are sensible measures, but they are not happening, again, because the gun controllers in Washington don't want compromise.

They want an issue. And the media want a fight to cheer on.

In the face of competing claims and the verbal barrage from Washington, the average citizen needs a way to separate fact from fiction, a way to see the real underlying issues, and the hidden goals of the gun lobby.

The next chapter offers the reader a kind of handbook on the issues, a place to thumb for answers whenever your neighbor, coworker, or spouse is misled into buying into the antigun propaganda.

Among other issues, the next chapter tells you the truth about

- terrorists and the supposed "gun-show loophole";
- why waiting periods are dangerous;
- the "cop-killer" bullets hoax;
- why gun "buybacks" are worse than useless;
- gun locks, safety, and citizen choice;
- the plastic gun sham;
- the "assault rifle" deceit;
- the Second Amendment and what it means today.

The third chapter addresses crime in America, explaining how our Second Amendment rights and stiff new laws against gun-toting criminals can extend and possibly accelerate the last decade's drop in crime.

The fourth chapter addresses terrorism, less of a threat to most Americans than crime, but a vector of danger that is widening. Since the AGS has brought it up, we've decided to take the issue seriously. This fourth chapter offers reasonable steps you can take to contribute to America's safety. And it shows how our Second Amendment rights can make America a little safer in the war against terror.

The fifth chapter is one we hope every gun owner will read. It addresses *real* gun safety, how America's moms and dads can make sure that our children are safe from our guns, just as we need those guns to keep us safe from criminals. It tells you what you need to know to get started, and leads gun owners to NRA materials and courses on gun safety.

Then we will take on the attacks from the gun-control lobby. We'll cover everything from fact-distorting historians to misguided philanthropists and trial lawyers looking to get rich by suing gun manufacturers into extinction. We'll take apart Hollywood hypocrites who lionize criminals—and would deny you the right to protect yourself from them. We'll show you the UN bureaucrats who want to internationalize gun control. And we'll expose the politicians who want to ride antigun hysteria into the White House.

The opposition to gun ownership from the big media, politicians, and legal eagles of the trial bar may seem like a monolithic force. It would be, were it not for the millions of American hunters and gun owners who understand our Constitution and its meaning far better than they do.

The war over guns is a war over truth. To be a gun owner in America today, you must also be armed with the facts. We must continue to be the men and women the Founders wished us to be.

Chapter Two

Your Handbook on Gun Issues

I don't think it's your right. . . . You are not allowed to own a gun, and if you do own a gun I think you should go to prison.

—*Rosie O'Donnell*

Pete Williams of NBC News has always given our side a fair break when it comes to covering gun issues.

So when Pete Williams asked one of the authors of this book, NRA executive vice president Wayne LaPierre, for a background interview about "assault rifles," it was too good an opportunity to turn down. LaPierre eagerly agreed.

LaPierre then made an invitation of his own, asking Williams to visit a shooting range with him a day before the interview. The purpose, he explained, would be to show him semi-automatic firearms, how they work, and why they really cannot be considered "assault rifles." Network news shows, when discussing the issue, often run video clips of fully automatic machine guns in their reports. These are intended to be disturbing images, scenes of staccato gunfire ripping up dummies or reducing target boards to shreds. The only problem is, fully automatic machine guns have been heavily restricted since the 1930s, and are simply irrelevant to the issue of semi-automatic firearms. After explaining this at the shooting range, LaPierre then showed Williams the kind of self-loading, semi-automatic hunting rifles that would be banned under the proposed law.

The next morning, when LaPierre turned on the television to watch his interview segment, he was disappointed to see the images running before viewers. How did the *Today* show introduce the segment?

You guessed it. With a video clip of an Al Capone–style machine gun blasting into the viewer's face. A red-faced Pete Williams later explained that the producers pick these clips, and they like to make them as spectacular as possible.

"Let's face it—the NRA is a punching bag for ratings on slow news days," says Chris Cox.

• • •

No one in the community of Second Amendment supporters need be surprised at this cavalier treatment of the issue by those NBC producers.

When a public policy group, the Media Research Center, tracked television coverage for two years in the late 1990s, it found that among 653 gun-policy stories broadcast, 357 stories tilted in favor of gun control. Only thirty-six tilted against gun control.[1] That's a bias factor of about ten-to-one—and frankly, we're surprised it's as good as that. Another factor is media sensationalism. In 1997, a year when crime fell nationwide by 4 percent across the board, the number of network news stories focusing on crime actually increased by 25 percent over the previous year.[2]

The problem originates not with the media, but with those who know how to manipulate it. The terms of the debate are set in a Buzzword Factory run by the antigun lobbies, funded by corporate foundations or the odd billionaire, and promoted by Hollywood celebrities and other elites far removed from the reality of the American streets.

These nongovernmental organizations (or NGOs, Washington-speak for issue-based nonprofit groups) hire consultants and Madison Avenue types who labor away in the Buzzword Factory with activists, invent new problems with gun ownership, and give it the most alarming name they can imagine.

These names then become the stuff of headlines for a pliant and uncritical media, from "assault rifles," to "gun-show loophole," to "plastic guns." In each instance, these descriptions are factually wrong. Never mind. They serve their purpose, and they do it well. They put supporters of the Second Amendment in the penalty box before the contest even begins.

To understand how this works, look at how other issues are treated. For example, editors would never dream of calling President Bush's economic legislation by its formal name. Referring to the Bush economic plan as the Economic Growth and Tax Relief Act would, rightly, make the press feel like partisan boosters. Yet when it comes to legislation from a self-styled maverick like John McCain, editors and producers uncritically refer to his legislation as "campaign finance reform." No wonder it passed. Even opponents of the legislation were cowed into calling this complex and controversial legislation by its deceptive title of "reform."

Now the success of "campaign finance reform" is leading to "Americans for Gun Safety." This new group is building on some old tricks that have their roots in the 1960s, with the shrill attack on "Saturday night specials."

"Gun safety" is just the latest. To do its job, any gun-control soundbite has to have three qualities:

• It must level alarmist accusations centered on largely nonexistent problems.

• It must announce a new emergency, one that paints supporters of the Second Amendment into a corner, making anyone who dares to question the need for immediate changes in the law sound like an extremist willing to risk lives for the sake of obscure principles.

• It must advance covert objectives aimed at making life more difficult for law-abiding gun owners.

In the pages that follow, we break down some of the most persistent of these "soundbite issues," beginning with the one that is at the heart of current efforts to control and restrict the ownership of guns in America—the so-called gun-show loophole. As you will see, the "gun-show loophole" is just one of the many soundbites that gun-control proponents have devised. After reading this chapter, you will be able to present the facts to someone who repeats one of these mantras from the great American gun-control Buzzword Factory.

The "Gun-Show Loophole": A Case Study in How to "Spin" a Problem That Does Not Exist

From our earliest days, Americans have liked to meet at gun shows where grown children take grandfather's hunting rifle, and collectors can find rare and beautiful antique firearms. If you believe the gun-control lobby, this age-old American institution has somehow mutated into a bazaar for violent felons, gangs, drug dealers, and now, they claim, international terrorists.

In fact, AGS claims to have "uncovered" several cases in which they allege suspected terrorists used gun shows to avoid background checks in Michigan, Florida, and Texas. "We are deluding ourselves if we believe that terrorists operating in America are adverse to using guns," says Jonathan Cowan, the former Clinton-Cuomo aide who runs AGS. "In fact, an Internet Web site urging Jihad against this country tells terrorists to acquire guns in America." AGS adds, "Given all the evidence we have about terrorists arming themselves in America, we can't continue to have an honor system for terrorists at gun shows."[3]

This would be alarming if it were true.

AGS Exploits America's Grief and Horror

Those who fret about the gun-show loophole strike the pose of reasonable people who just want to address a worrisome defect in national gun laws.

The truth is, AGS documents show that Mr. Cowan and company (assisted by a former Clinton political aide and a former gun advisor to Senator Chuck Schumer, the leader of the gun-ban corps in the Senate) are using AGS to advance their "top national priority... passage of licensing and/or registration in the next Congress."[4]

In other words, they want every gun owner in America to be subject to harsh new laws that can only ultimately lead to confiscation (as you'll see in the section below, "California, Canada, and Confiscation"). "I grew up around gun shows," says the NRA's Chris Cox. "I don't ever recall seeing jet fuel, anthrax, or even boxcutters." Certainly, AGS's use of America's grief and horror in the wake of the September 11 attacks doesn't hold up.

Inventing Terrorists

AGS wants to inject "terrorism" into the firearm policy debate at any cost, and it is willing to employ serial lies to forge a link between "terrorist" cases and gun shows. AGS rests one of these cases not on the Middle East, but on Ireland. AGS continues to cite the case of an "IRA terrorist" even though the jury that convicted the man for firearm violations acquitted him of the specific charge that he was an IRA terrorist. It is also clear from the record that the guns in question were bought at gun shows by "straw" purchasers (people with "clean" records who are willing to violate federal law and illegally purchase firearms on behalf of criminals prohibited from doing so). Nothing in the legislation AGS is promoting would or could prevent people from breaking the law in this way.

And remember Ali Boumelhem from the first chapter, who AGS says attended a Detroit-area gun show so he could ship guns to Lebanon? Convicted one day before the September 11 attacks of conspiring to smuggle guns and ammunition, he has become an AGS poster boy to spread the lie that gun shows are a steady source of guns for foreign terrorists. The truth is that after the FBI placed this convicted felon under surveillance, he was arrested, prosecuted, and convicted in federal court—proving that existing firearms laws can work. To suggest that he slipped through a "gun-show loophole" is misleading at best. Once again, the best evidence shows that this convicted felon worked through a straw purchaser. That's not a loophole. That's a crime. Again, nothing in the McCain "gun-show loophole" bill or any other proposal would prevent such an illegal act.

AGS also trotted out the case of a Texas man—but investigations failed to show he had any connection to any terrorist attacks. There is now no indication to believe that he ever shipped guns overseas or bought guns for any reason other than personal protection.

One thing is for sure. If terrorists come to America determined to find guns, they can do so, just like common street thugs. They may find some way to subvert the law and obtain their firearms from a gun show or a gun store. It is more likely that they will obtain their guns in the same manner criminals do every day, from other criminals.

Or they will bring them with them.

Throughout the heartland of terrorism in the Middle East, one can walk into many *souks* and find an astonishing array of firearms—machine guns, bazookas, and other weapons that are illegal or heavily restricted in the United States. For a terrorist to come to a gun show in America looking for weapons makes about as much sense as an American going to Peshawar looking for a bake sale.

Gun shows today are much more likely to attract undercover agents from the Bureau of Alcohol, Tobacco and Firearms, the FBI, and the state police than Middle Eastern terrorists. There simply is no national security case to be made to crack down on this beloved American institution.

What the Law Really Says: There Is *No* Gun-Show Loophole

The gun controllers conveniently forget to mention the most important aspect of each of their examples. In every case, the system worked. The violators were arrested, tried, and convicted.

What does the law say now? *Convicted felons face a possible ten-year prison sentence just for touching a gun at a gun show. Federal law already prohibits nonresident and illegal aliens from buying guns.*

Unlike the infamous cash-and-carry arms bazaars of the Middle East, licensed dealers at U.S. gun shows must perform the same background checks and fill out the same federal forms as they do when selling a gun in a store. Anyone who is in the business of selling firearms must obtain a Federal Firearms License from the BATF. That's the law already.

Fiction: Gun-control groups claim that 50 percent to 75 percent of guns used in crimes come from gun shows.

Fact: A 1997 National Institute of Justice study reported that only 2 percent of criminal guns came from gun shows. Another report in that year by the U.S. Bureau of Justice Statistics on federal firearms offenders reported that only 1.7 percent of guns used in crime were acquired at a gun show. Numerous other studies came to these same, fractional results—and in many of these cases, the criminals used straw purchasers. The fact is, gun shows are open, friendly, and public. They provide the kind of well-lit attention criminals do not like.[5]

Still, there must be something that the gun controllers can hang their hats on, right?

Here it is. In the 1990s, a National Instant Check System (NICS) went into effect, a computerized database of people with criminal records who are disqualified from acquiring firearms. Under instant check, dealers must clear every firearms purchase through a background check with the FBI. Each dealer is given a Federal Firearms License number, a unique password, and information on the prospective buyer—name, date of birth, sex, and race (why the federal government should record that is anyone's guess), as well as the type of gun sought.

An operator checks the data against the instant check database. If you are not a prohibited person, you get your gun. If the check turns up ambiguous information (maybe someone else with your name in your state who has a criminal record), an analyst looks over the data. By law, the analyst has to approve or deny the sale within three business days, or the purchase may proceed.

The majority of gun-show sellers are licensed dealers. By law, they must conduct these checks.

However, this requirement for federal licensing and the background check does not extend to people who occasionally sell or trade guns from their personal collections. This is not a loophole. This is an acknowledgment that people like to trade and sell guns, just as they like to hold garage sales. Congress made sure that the widow selling her husband's hunting rifle or the collector ogling that Winchester rifle with the stock of Swedish pine would not have to bear the fees, wait, and paperwork burden of filling out Federal Firearm Licenses with the BATF if they get together on their own to make a deal.

Congress wisely recognized that people will do this. Hunters sell guns from their homes, through classified ads, and at their clubs and ranges. A gun show is just a place for them to meet. Outlaw these transactions in ordinary, everyday commerce, and you won't be doing anything to make life harder for criminals. Remember, gun commerce by violent criminals, drug dealers, fugitives, and illegal aliens is already a crime. Simple gun possession by a prohibited person is already a federal felony punishable by ten years in the federal slammer.

By putting all private sales under the heavy hand of the government, the gun-control lobby seeks to criminalize millions of law-abiding Americans.

That, of course, is their intent: to criminalize so they can control.

Death by Red Tape

The "reforms" proposed by Senators McCain and Lieberman would not reduce crime. But they would be very effective in killing the great American gun show.

They do this by intentionally proposing a system that would be utterly unworkable. For example, suppose you go to a gun show and see a Colt that you want to add to your collection. But money's tight that month, so you decide against buying. Six months later, you get a tax refund and decide to spend it. You remember that you wrote down the seller's name, so you call her. Yes, it turns out she does happen to still have that old Colt.

But McCain's legislation would prohibit you from buying the gun directly from the purchaser. This is worse than onerous. And that is the point—once again, to shut down all private gun commerce.

The truth is, any realistic, enforceable background check requirement must be limited to sales at an actual gun show, to guns that are present at that show. And the background check must be conducted in an expedient and timely fashion.

Added to McCain's requirement is a move to force gun-show promoters into one of two tiers, as either "frequent" or "infrequent" types of "special firearms event operators." The point is to create more forms, more fees, more hassles—and fewer gun shows. Moreover, many anti–gun show proposals would require you, even if you do not come to the show with a gun or buy a gun, to provide information about your identity to be recorded by the show operator. Federal agencies would be allowed to retain these records, as well your instant check records.

Similar legislation proposed by Senators Frank Lautenberg and Jack Reed defines a gun show so broadly that it would include any form of nonretail sales. Under these proposals, your living room could become a "gun show." Merely offering to "exchange" a firearm at an "event" would be banned. This means that your local gun club's Sunday trap shoot would be such an "event" and subject to rigorous provisions. Make a mistake, and you could spend years in prison.

Death by Delay

So what we offered them was, "OK, twenty-four hours for everyone you can check within twenty-four hours, but—over 90 percent of them you can check in twenty-four hours. But for those you can't check, because there's some problem with it, we ought to be able to hold them up for three days."

—*President Bill Clinton, ABC's* This Week, *March 12, 2000*

During his presidency, Bill Clinton proposed a deeper check against mental records that would not, he said, hold up most people. He compared it to airport metal detectors and called it a "little inconvenience to preserve the public safety."

This proposal, of course, remains on the wish list of the gun-control lobby. To make such a privacy-intrusive check, they say, would take three days (not including weekends and holidays). In other words, it would take as long as needed to outlast the gun show. In a moment of candor, Democratic House leaders put out a letter on Capitol Hill saying they would accept nothing less than legislation, like the Lautenberg bill, *that would make gun shows unworkable.*

The Instant Check Scandal

The NRA supports a quick, efficient, and effective background check of retail gun purchases. At the state level, we've worked closely with legislators to write laws requiring computerized instant criminal records checks on purchasers of firearms—seventeen states have such laws—and for those who carry firearms for protection in public.

The dirty secret of the gun-control lobby is that they do not want effective background checks on retail gun sales. The administration of President Clinton was allocated $300 million to make the instant check system workable. There's no telling where that money went.[6] It did not bring the system up to the standard easily obtained by private-sector companies like American Express or VISA. Now the Bush administration is scrambling to make the National Instant Check System worthy of the name.

The General Accounting Office reported that between 1995 and September 1999, the NICS went dark 360 times, amounting to more than 215 hours of downtime. That's 215 hours during which the retail sales of guns were, effectively, banned in the United States.[7] Even more shocking is the fact that the system failed to provide instant checks 28 percent of the time, delaying sales for 1.2 million legal purchasers from hours to days. (Imagine how long VISA could stay in business if it treated customers like that.)[8] Here's the most disturbing news—3,353 felons and others prohibited by law from purchasing firearms were allowed to buy guns over the counter after being mistakenly approved by NICS. Yet only 3.3 percent of these prohibited individuals were being investigated by the federal government. *Why wouldn't the federal government follow up on leads which clearly showed that people who shouldn't be near a gun were walking around with them?*[9]

The McCain-Lieberman proposal promises ultimately to allow only a twenty-four-hour check. Sounds reasonable. But the legislation offers the federal government and states no real incentives to improve the availability of computerized records. The legislation proposes a three-business-day window to verify out-of-state records. A few large states would bring down the whole system.

H. Sterling Burnett, a senior policy analyst at the nonpartisan National Center for Policy Analysis, surveyed gun-show legislation and concluded: "Rather than expanding the flawed NICS [instant check] to cover the small number of private sales at gun shows, money could be better spent fixing the NICS and prosecuting the felons who have already purchased guns illegally."[10]

Why, then, would anyone be opposed to making background checks work? If you have to ask this question, you still don't get it. You still do not understand the mindset of the gun-control lobby. The point is *not* to catch criminals. The point is to criminalize, measure by measure, the ownership of guns in America.

California, Canada, and Confiscation

"Governments that register guns can confiscate guns."

That is a mantra of ours. And we say it knowing that it will strike many people as a paranoid statement, especially when put against the benign, hunter-friendly image of groups like AGS.

All we ask is that people consider the evidence. Gun registration—after similarly benign explanations to gun owners—did lead to confiscation in Canada, Great Britain, and California. Canada and Great Britain are two countries with our same sense of individual rights; two countries in which every home should be a castle; two countries dedicated to maximum personal liberty. California is the most populous state in our country.

Three places—among many others—where gun registration has led to gun confiscation.

Canada Lie

Canada provides the most frightening example, because it is the country in the world most like us. Same frontier culture. Same background in hunting and sportsmanship.

On a February day in 1995, Allan Rock, then Canadian justice minister, declared to the people of Canada: "Let us not hear that [registration] is a prelude to the confiscation by the government of hunting rifles and shotguns.... There is no reason to confiscate legally owned firearms."[11]

It took all of ten months for Parliament to break this promise by passing the Canadian Firearms Act, which used registration records to confiscate legally owned firearms.

The first provision to go into effect banned private ownership of well more than half of Canada's legally registered pistols, more than 553,000 legally registered handguns—any handgun of .32 or .25 caliber, and any handgun with a barrel length of 105mm (4.14 inches) or less. Pistol owners were given a choice of selling their guns to those legally allowed to buy them (a patent Catch-22 that made this option no real option at all), or rendering them inoperable, or surrendering their guns to the government without compensation.[12] The new law also requires a government-issued firearms owner license. A Canadian who owns a shotgun or rifle but who failed to apply for a license faces five years in prison and a $2,000 fine. These licenses are also required to buy a long gun, and even apply to boxes of rifle cartridges.[13] The law also requires each individual long gun to be registered by 2003. It's pretty easy to see where that registration is going to lead.[14]

Again, cracking down on crime is not the intent of this legislation. Cracking down on law-abiding Canadian gun owners is.

The government's own records show that since the first handgun registry was passed in 1934, not one single crime has been solved in Canada using the national pistol registry. The Canadian government estimates that a gun is used for self-protection 32,000 times a year in Canada. Analyzing these numbers, the Canadian Institute for Legislative Action estimates that "approximately forty lives are saved for every life lost with a firearm in Canada." That same institute found that 44 percent of rural Canadian households own firearms, compared to 11 percent in cities. Yet the violent crime rate in Canadian cities is 40 percent higher than in rural areas.

If the government in Ottawa were concerned about crime, it would enthusiastically permit gun ownership. Once again, we see that confiscation—not crime—is the real concern.[15]

Not So Great Britain

The American right to keep and bear arms can trace its origins to British common law. For centuries, a rifle over the hearth symbolized a vision of the English home as a personal "keep." As new factions gained power in the early twentieth century, however, the ideals of Rudyard Kipling gave way to the ideals of Fabian socialism.

The Firearms Act of 1920 trampled on this ancient right. Suddenly, citizens could possess rifles and pistols only if they could prove they had "good reason" for receiving a police permit—a "firearms certificate." Self-defense, at that time, was considered a "good reason."

In the 1990s, the restrictions on gun ownership were tightened in reaction to a rampage shooting in an elementary school in Scotland by a madman. Guns of any sort are almost impossible to obtain or keep in Great Britain.

Are the British any safer now that they've jettisoned this aspect of their individual liberty?

A British think tank, the Centre for Defence Studies at King's College, looked at gun crime and concluded that criminal use of handguns increased 40 percent in the two years *after* British authorities confiscated all legally owned handguns from private hands. A former head of the firearm research division of New Scotland Yard found that

• licensing law-abiding gun ownership doesn't deter criminals from having guns;

• firearms robberies *rose* following the handgun ban;

• "the short-term impact [of the handgun ban] strongly suggests that there is no direct link between the unlawful use of handguns and their lawful ownership."[16]

While criminals are having a field day, the isolated, rural farmer who uses a gun to protect himself from being marauded is treated like a criminal. In fact, he is a criminal. Incredibly, people who use guns in the most extreme cases of self-defense are being tried for first-degree murder in Great Britain.

Australia, also in response to a rampage shooting by a madman, similarly cracked down on gun ownership by law-abiding citizens. The result, predictably, is reports of escalating gun violence in Australia's urban centers.

California Scheming

The logic of closing the nonexistent gun-show loophole, says the analyst Burnett, is to "lead to calls for closing other nonexistent loopholes until all private firearms transfers—even those between family and friends—are under government regulation."[17]

Welcome to California, long heralded as the American future. Legislators in the Golden State have already banned all private gun sales. For each gun sale, licensed gun dealers have to submit to a two-week waiting period, pay a substantial fee, and register the sale with the California Department of Justice.

It is easy to see where California—the nation's most populous state—is heading. It is the beachhead for registration—and confiscation—in America. The United States is fast becoming the last place on earth you can legally buy and own guns. And that right is shrinking before our eyes.

The record is clear: *Gun registration leads to gun confiscation.*

Why Waiting Periods Are Dangerous

Waiting-period proposals go back to the early days of the antigun issue in the 1960s. The theory is simple. A "cooling off" period is needed to prevent angry people from stomping down to a gun dealer, buying a gun, and committing a crime of passion.

Waiting-period proponents tried, but failed, to make these delays part of the law in 1993. Why did such a reasonable-sounding proposal languish? Simple. Proponents just could not put forward *any* evidence that supported their theory. Instead, Congress chose to go in the other direction and pass the instant check concept.

If anything, the empirical evidence bears out that waiting periods are dangerous. California imposed a fifteen-day waiting period on firearms sales in 1975 (reduced to ten days in 1977). What was the result?

California's violent crime rate was 50 percent higher each year, on average, compared to the rest of the country. A Library of Congress study concluded, "It is difficult to find a correlation between the existence of strict firearms regulations and a lower incidence of gun-related crimes."[18]

In fact, waiting periods may be subtle incubators of crime. After all, waiting periods do not stop criminals. They do, however, stop law-abiding citizens from obtaining access to firearms when they need them. Like unreasonable fees and taxes, waiting periods are a form of rationing that often comes down hardest on those who need protection the most.

You could be a woman afraid of a stalker. A shop owner threatened by goons looking for protection money or a homeowner worried by a spate of robberies on your street. For whatever reason, if you feel your life is suddenly in danger and you live in a state with waiting periods, you might have to hide under the bed or under a counter for a good ten days.

And be real quiet.

The "Cop-Killer" Bullet Hoax

The "cop-killer" bullet: This is an old saw that gun-controlling politicians like Barbara Boxer and Chuck Schumer keep trying to resurrect. It certainly deserves a mention in the Buzzword Factory hall of fame for its imaginative use of brazen mistruths.

The bottom line: *The Bureau of Alcohol, Tobacco, and Firearms reported to Congress in 1997 that* no *law-enforcement officer has ever been killed or injured because an armor-piercing bullet penetrated a bullet-resistant vest.*

Despite a lack of evidence that there was a threat from "cop-killer" bullets, NRA leaders long ago responded to public concern. In the 1980s we informed legislators about the characteristics of the bullets being discussed, and helped shaped legislation. We also met with the U.S. Treasury Department to help draft regulations. As a result, it is illegal to manufacture and import, for private use, handgun bullets made of special, hard metals. In 1994, the law was amended to include specially jacketed bullets invented for use by law enforcement and military personnel. That should have been the end of this issue. Since then the Clinton-Gore administration called for legislation—similar to proposals opposed by the Departments of Treasury and Justice, and rejected by Congress in the 1980s—that would have practically outlawed all rifle ammunition used by hunters and a wide variety of handgun ammunition traditionally used for sport and self-defense.

Gun-control groups continue to mislead the public about the danger to law-enforcement officers. BATF reported that no new laws were needed. In fact, BATF appealed to Congress on the need to "avoid experimentation with police officer lives that could conceivably lead to numerous officer fatalities."

Those who would ban cop-killer bullets would ban virtually all rifle bullets. There are no "cop-killer" bullets. There are, however, Second Amendment–killing proposals that hide behind media-friendly buzzwords.

Gun "Buybacks": Worse Than Useless

In fact, the studies published by the Justice Department demonstrate that gun buy-back programs have "no effect" on crime and that more background checks at gun shows could affect only 2 percent of criminals' guns used in crime.

—*Senator Jeff Sessions*, Washington Times, *May 15, 2000*

Cities around the United States have spent fortunes on programs to buy guns and then destroy them. The term gun "buyback" is a misnomer, since people don't buy guns from the government. The phrase itself is a kind of Freudian slip for those who believe firearms should be only government property.

Consider the case of Washington, D.C., scene of the nation's highest homicide rate in the late 1990s. In 1998, the city managed to lock up only two criminals for breaking federal gun laws. But all it had to do to convince a friendly media that it was cracking down on crime was to pay residents $100 for guns turned in for destruction over two summer days. Bill Clinton was in the White House then, and clearly appreciated the feel-good potential of this program. He sought to spend more than $15 million of the taxpayers' money on programs for other cities. These gun turn-ins continue to be a popular but misguided drain on public budgets.

Dr. Gary Kleck, a Florida State University criminologist, believes that such programs are worse than a waste of money. They won't stop crime—most of the people who turn in guns are women and senior citizens, who are least likely to commit crimes of violence. Worse, because they offer a "no-questions-asked" policy, they provide robbers and murderers with a legal way to dispense with a crime-scene gun—and get paid for it!

Indeed, it is likely that, far from stemming the supply of guns, gun turn-ins actually *increase* the supply of guns. George Mason University law professor Daniel D. Polsby noted: "It is implausible that these schemes will actually result in a less-dangerous population. Government programs to buy surplus cheese cause more cheese to be produced without affecting the availability of cheese to people who want to buy it. So it is with guns."[19]

For a criminal, the bounties paid by city governments actually encourage the surrender of cheaper, small-caliber handguns, providing a subsidy to replace them with larger-caliber, more powerful guns. Moreover, in a crime-ravaged inner city, these bounties clearly subsidize the stealing of guns in order to sell them. Indeed, they put city governments in the position of acting *as a fence for gun thieves*.

Gun Locks and Safety: A Matter of Citizen Choice

When seven children were wounded in an apparently gang-related shooting at the National Zoo in Washington, D.C., then vice president Al Gore took a stand for mandatory gun locks.

He meant to advance the cause of gun control. In fact, he could not have done a more effective job in highlighting the dubious link between gun locks and crime. After all, who would believe gun locks could prevent gang-related shootings?

Nevertheless, proposals were made that would make gun locks mandatory and would hold ordinary citizens liable for the crimes committed by criminals with stolen guns. In the process, the Buzz-word Factory turned such locks into "child-safety locks."

It then became the responsibility of those of us who know guns and understand how they work to make a reasonable objection. Our objection, of course, immediately drew high-dudgeon moral outrage from the gun-control crowd. Who could be against mandatory "child-safety locks"?

We could.

In fact, the NRA—as an organization that understands guns and how they operate—had a moral obligation to speak out. We had to let it be known that a mandatory trigger lock would be an approach guaranteed to *cost* lives.

Don't get us wrong. The NRA supported legislation to make gun locks available to all purchasers at the point of sale—a proposal that is law today. And we stand squarely for gun safety in the home. Indeed, we support the laws (on the books in every state) that mandate that guns be stored properly. Adults who are grossly negligent in leaving firearms sitting about the house are open to felony charges in many parts of the country—and we support that as well.

But like most "one size fits all" solutions, mandatory gun locks are not the best solution for everyone in every place. They are not right for the single woman living alone, the elderly couple, the owner of an inner-city hotel who never knows if the next person through the door is a paying customer or a crackhead.

The Problem with Trigger Locks

If I'm a bad guy, I'm always gonna have a gun. Safety locks? You will pull the trigger with the lock on, and I'll pull the trigger. We'll see who wins.

—*Salvatore "Sammy the Bull" Gravano,*
Vanity Fair, *September 1999*

Trigger Locks Are Not Foolproof: A trigger lock is a mechanism installed on the inside of a gun's trigger guard. Like any mechanism made to fit into another, it can operate imperfectly.

• One prominent gun company warns against putting its gun lock on a loaded gun. When tested, its handguns did indeed fire. Other handgun models did as well. Trigger locks could easily lead to a false sense of security, costing lives—just as the introduction of child safety caps on prescription drugs *increased* child poisonings.

• When the U.S. Consumer Product Safety Commission tested dozens of locks, it found only two that met its standards.[20]

• One gun company had to recall 750,000 trigger locks because of defects.[21]

• Researchers have found that common gun locks can be opened with tweezers or paper clips or by dropping them. They found that gun locks will not stop a determined teenager or adult.[22]

Trigger Locks Can Aid Criminals: Most damning of all was a demonstration by Parris Glendening, the liberal governor of Maryland who championed a bill mandating gun locks. The governor held a press conference in the spring of 2000 to demonstrate how easy these locks are to put on a gun. He then proceeded to fumble with the lock for a full minute, jerking and pushing and flushing with embarrassment. Another agonizing minute went by, while chuckling and murmured disbelief spread through the press corps. Even Glendening's heir apparent as governor—Lieutenant Governor Kathleen Kennedy Townsend—had to turn her head to hide an embarrassed smirk.

Finally, a state trooper came to the governor's rescue and showed him how to open the lock. Now consider, the governor is a former college professor and was in a well-lit room and under no threat of physical harm. And yet manipulating the lock was beyond his ability.[23]

Again, the NRA supports trigger locks and other means to make guns inaccessible to children. However, we have a moral obligation to object to laws that mandate one solution for all people, especially when that solution is technically problematic in so many situations.

The Glendening story is funny. Perhaps we ought to mandate the provision of a Maryland state trooper with the sale of every gun lock. Of course, this is not a laughing matter for the woman who has considerably less than two minutes to stop an intruder breaking into her house.

Firearm Safety in America

Gun-control groups make inflated claims of the numbers of children who are killed in gun accidents. To achieve their alarming statistics, they factor in teenagers (including many gang-related shootings) and adults under age twenty-four.

To achieve your arms around the issue of safety, you first must know the facts. We put together some data from the National Center for Health Statistics, the Centers for Disease Control and Prevention, the National Center for Injury Prevention and Control, the National Safety Council, and other groups.[24]

• The evidence shows that firearm deaths are at an all-time low, especially among children. So is the fatal firearm accident rate, which has declined 91 percent since the all-time high in 1904, *50 percent during the decade 1989 to 1998.*[25]

• Among children, firearm accidents account for 2 percent of accidental deaths. An American child is much more likely to die because of a motor vehicle accident, drowning, fall, fire, choking, or poisoning, or a physician's medical mistake.[26]

• Since 1930, the American population has more than doubled and the number of guns has quintupled. Yet the annual number of firearm-related deaths has decreased 73 percent.

Conclusion: Accidental firearm deaths are at an all-time low, while gun ownership is at an all-time high.

Still, no one should be complacent about the issue of child safety. The inflated claims of the antigun lobby aside, the real number of children killed by accidental firearm-related deaths in 1998 was 121.[27] It has been estimated that the number of lives saved by private gun ownership is more than seventy times the number of lives lost, including this small number of accidents.[28] Still, those 121 young lives were exactly 121 too many.

What can we do to drive these numbers toward zero?

First, we must realize that government regulation has played *no* role in decreasing firearm accidents. You can see this in the logic of the antigun crowd's argument. If they are right, the quintupling of privately owned guns should have at least quintupled the number of accidental deaths, not decreased it. Much of this decrease occurred in decades in which there was no gun control. The decrease continues today when a majority of states have instituted concealed-carry laws.

So what is going on here?

Gun accidents are decreasing because of education. No one has done more to make gun owners safety-conscious than the NRA. In the last decade alone, the NRA has spent $100 million on gun safety, with $20 million going to our Eddie Eagle GunSafe program, which has reached fifteen million children through 20,000 schools, civic groups, and law-enforcement agencies.[29] Every year, the NRA's 38,000 Certified Instructors and Coaches train 700,000 people a year in gun safety.[30]

Only you can assess your personal situation. You should decide the safest way of storing a gun yourself. One thing is for sure: when it comes to safety, one size doesn't fit all.

If you are a parent concerned about gun safety, Chapter Five has the information and links to get you started.

The Plastic Gun Sham

Plastic guns: This is the Buzzword Factory at its most ingenious. It all started back in 1986 with a syndicated column by Jack Anderson that reported that gun markets were being inundated with "plastic guns" that would pass freely through airport metal detectors. Even worse, it was reported, Libya's Muammar al-Qaddafi put in an order to buy three thousand of them.

Now, almost twenty years later, after boxcutters have been used to transform civilian airliners into kamikaze bombs, the need for airport security could not be clearer. Plastic guns? Who could be in favor of that?

The report originated from the antigun lobby's ceaseless Buzzword Factory in response to the Glock 17's revolutionary new handgun design that used lightweight polymers in the frame and handle.

Gun-rights supporters were stunned by the way in which this story was picked up by an uncritical media and used to inflame the public. We knew: *There is no such thing as a plastic gun.*

And what about the Glocks that were at the center of the controversy? These excellent, compact, lightweight Austrian-made handguns incorporate eighteen ounces of steel (about 83 percent of its total weight)—making them fully detectable by airport security. Phillip McGuire, associate director of law enforcement of the BATF, testified to Congress: "The entire issue was raised in response to reports, many wildly inaccurate, concerning a particular firearm, the Glock 17."[31]

Billie Vincent, former FAA director of Civil Aviation Security, testified: "[D]espite a relatively common impression to the contrary, there is no current non-metal firearm which is not reasonably detectable by present technology and methods in use at our airports today, nor to my knowledge is anyone on the threshold of developing such a firearm."[32]

The Libya connection also turned out to be somebody's misinformation.

Of course, these facts did not matter. By the time the media realized they had once again been had, this issue had become a steamroller, culminating in legislative proposals that would have banned millions of commonplace handguns. Common sense tells any gun owner that any firearm design will, by necessity, have detectable amounts of metal; the metal is needed to contain the enormous pressure of firing a cartridge. But no one can guarantee the future. For that reason, the NRA backed the Hughes-McCollum bill. Signed into law by President Reagan, this bill makes illegal the development and production of any firearm that is undetectable by airport detectors.

Despite this, some in the gun-control lobby continue to lie. They will continue to tell you that plastic guns are legal. And they will tell you that the NRA supports plastic guns.

Their approach seems simple. When you can't win on the facts, just lie. Do it often enough and the media will believe you.

The "Assault Rifle" Deceit: Making Guns Politically Correct

> If I could have gotten fifty-one votes in the Senate of the United States for an outright ban, picking up every one of them, "Mr. and Mrs. America, turn them all in," I would have done it.
> —*Senator Dianne Feinstein, CBS's* 60 Minutes, *February 5, 1995*

Anyone questioning whether registration equals confiscation should consider the way in which California politicians broke their word to law-abiding citizens. The state attorney general offered Californians a deadline extension for registering semi-automatic rifles. Many were surprised to see how they were treated when they registered.

"These gun owners trusted the government—with their good name and the fact that they owned an item of personal property—and that trust was broken," says Sandra Froman, California native and NRA second vice president. "Ultimately," she continued, "they either had to move that personal property out of state, give it to the state, or have it forcibly taken by the state and face prosecution."[33]

What Is an "Assault Weapon"?
The development and marketing of the so-called "assault weapon" concept is another Buzzword Factory hall-of-famer.

simply referring to semi-automatic firearms. They rely, as the NBC
producers did, on scaring the public by blurring the distinction
between a fully automatic firearm—a machine gun—and a semi-
automatic. The tactic is revealed as purely intentional. Back in 1988,
Josh Sugarmann, of the Violence Policy Center, let the cat out of the
bag with a primer for gun-control activists.

He said that the "issue of handgun restriction remains a non-issue
with the vast majority of legislators, the press, and public. . . . Assault
weapons . . . are a new topic. The weapons' menacing looks, coupled
with the public's confusion over fully automatic machine guns ver-
sus semi-automatic assault weapons—anything that looks like a
machine gun is assumed to be a machine gun—can only increase the
chance of public support for restrictions on these weapons.[34]

Unlike machine guns, semi-automatics fire only once each time
the trigger is pulled. The semi-automatic action merely refers to a
mechanism that uses the energy from a fired round to eject the
empty case of the fired round and reload a fresh round into the
firearm's chamber. These firearms use the same ammunition as
other firearms.

The first semi-automatic was produced in 1885. Theodore Roosevelt, American president and NRA life member, hunted with a
semi-automatic. But he wasn't the only president to do so. Ironically, at the same time he was urging Congress to enact a ban on
certain semi-automatic firearms, President Bill Clinton took a very
public bird-hunting trip to Maryland's eastern shore, presumably
to prove his pro-hunting credentials to skeptical sportsmen. On
that much photographed trip, the president used a Benelli Field
Auto Shotgun, a firearm that with just a few cosmetic alterations—
such as the addition of a collapsible stock and pistol grip—would
be banned under the very legislation he was pushing. Today, Americans own about thirty million semi-automatic rifles, pistols, and
shotguns (about 15 percent of all privately owned firearms in the
United States).[35]

Criminals Do Not Use Semi-Automatics

Americans love semi-automatics because they are convenient for hunting and target shooting, and because they make skeet, trap, and sporting clays easier and more fun to shoot. Semi-automatic firearms, including some affected by the federal "assault weapons" laws, are highly valued by gun collectors. Semi-automatic handguns are used in formal marksmanship competitions.

Criminals, however, have a decided bias against these types of firearms. FBI data show that rifles of any type are used in only 3 percent of homicides.[36] State and local police reports indicate that less than 1 percent of violent crimes are committed with so-called assault weapons. Criminologist Gary Kleck has determined that less than 0.5 percent of all violent crimes involve assault weapons. In Washington, D.C., for example, out of 3,600 homicides surveyed between 1985 and 1994, not a single one involved any kind of rifle.

If these rifles are not used in crimes, why, then, do the media and politicians persist in calling them "assault weapons"?

The Conversion Myth

Whenever you pin down gun-control professionals on the facts about "assault weapons," they shift their claim to a new one—that semi-automatics are easy to convert into fully automatic weapons. They would have you believe that millions of firearms in gun racks across America are just waiting a snip, a clip, and a slap to turn them into fully automatic machine guns.

So they focus on the minutiae, seeking ever tighter regulations of common features of many legal guns, from detachable magazines, to flash suppressors, to folding stocks, to bayonet lugs. What it all boils down to is this:

• Any firearm that would be "easy to convert" into a fully automatic would not be approved by the BATF for sale to the general public.

• Any firearm part "designed and intended . . . for use in converting" a firearm into a machine gun is restricted under federal law. If someone possesses an illegally converted machine gun, or an illegal conversion part, they would be committing a federal felony punishable by ten years in prison and $10,000 in fines.[37]

Focus on Crime, Not Hardware

While rifles of any type are used in 3 percent of all homicides, knives are used in 13 percent, bare hands in 5 percent, and blunt objects in 4 percent of all killings. The annual number of homicides committed with rifles has declined 36 percent since 1980. They are the type of firearm least likely to be used in a crime.[38]

FBI statistics show that in the decade prior to 1993, 73 percent of persons identified in the felonious killing of police officers had prior criminal arrests, 56 percent had prior convictions, 23 percent were on probation or parole at the time of the killing, and 5 percent had prior murder arrests.[39]

Clearly, if a fraction of the interest focused on bayonet lugs and folding stocks had been diverted to keeping violent criminals in prison longer, many police officers lost to violence would be walking their beats today.

One favorite case study for the gun-control lobby is that of Buford Furrow, an anti-Semite with ties to hate groups who went on a rampage in the North Valley Jewish Community Center, in Granada Hills, California.

The media went into orbit that he used a firearm. More important, however, was the fact that he was a convicted felon with a history of psychopathic behavior. He had previously been hauled before a Washington State judge for violating probation by possessing a firearm. Yet nobody in authority, certainly not the Clinton Justice Department, bothered to follow up on his *illegal possession* of a firearm—*which constituted a federal felony*. Enforcing the existing law could have kept him off the street; banning semi-automatics, on the other hand, would not have stopped this terrorist from finding a weapon.[40]

The Real Intent Behind the Law

When President Clinton signed the federal "Crime Bill" into law in 1994, it included provisions to make it illegal to possess or transfer certain types of "assault weapons." These included semi-automatic rifles equipped with a detachable magazine and two or more attachments (such as a bayonet lug or flash suppressor), as well as handguns and shotguns with similar characteristics. The manufacture of ammunition magazines holding more than ten cartridges was also outlawed.

However, the law "grandfathered" those guns and magazines made before September 13, 1994. What happened next was entirely predictable. In anticipation of the gun ban, many manufacturers accelerated production to boost legal inventories. After the ban, the BATF informed manufacturers that they could continue to produce firearms identical to "assault weapons," provided they lacked the prohibited features. The media hype interested many Americans in this particular configuration of firearm, and buyer interest naturally surges in any product soon to become illegal.

So in the interest of advancing gun control, it is likely that there are now more of these rifles and "high-capacity" magazines in private hands today.

You might wonder, why did gun-control advocates bother with all of this bureaucratic nonsense? The answer was provided in an editorial in the pro–gun control *Washington Post*, which said: "No one should have any illusions about what was accomplished [by the ban]. Assault weapons play a part in only a small percentage of crime. The provision is mainly symbolic; its virtue will be if it turns out to be, as hoped, a stepping stone to broader gun control."[41]

The current law governing "assault weapons" is scheduled to expire in September 2004—just in time to become a political issue for the next presidential election. You can bet that by then the Buzzword Factory will have found a way to cast the debate on fresh terms, based on a new "crisis." In Chapter Eleven, we will look at the political challenges of this looming debate.

Ballistic Fingerprinting: Registration by Another Name

One proposal gaining in popularity is the marking of cartridges, so that spent shells at a crime scene can be directly tied to the gun—

and presumably its owner. This is often portrayed as a common-sense way to allow law enforcement to make the most of forensic evidence at the scene.

The NRA is all in favor of helping law enforcement. But how effective is ballistic fingerprinting? First of all, given that many guns used in crimes are stolen, ballistic fingerprinting would only connect lawful gun owners to crimes they did not commit. Worse, the technology has not proven to be an effective use of scarce human and budgetary resources. The State of Maryland enacted ballistic fingerprinting, spending $6 million on technology and throwing in the services of a dozen state troopers to key in entries and track data.

How many matches has this technology been able to make between criminals and crimes? A big fat zero.

However, the Maryland law did effectively ban handgun sales for months, since manufacturers were not equipped to instantly retool their production lines to meet the needs of this law. And it is one way to effectively resist gun owners. After all, what's the difference between being fingerprinted and being "ballistically fingerprinted"?

As a form of gun control, ballistic fingerprinting works. As a form of crime control, it flunks. Ballistic fingerprinting diverts the services of good law-enforcement officers from crime fighting to data processing.

.50-Caliber Ban: Cracking Down on Antiques

Any criminals reading this, please note: .50-caliber rifles cost thousands of dollars, measure four to five feet in length, weigh twenty-two to thirty-four pounds, and are . . . well . . . just a tad difficult to tuck in your belt and hide under a raincoat before holding up a bank or liquor store.

For more than a century, however, these rifles have been favored by long-range target-shooting experts, including those who cherish such venerable antiques as Winchesters, Sharps, and Maynards. Gun collectors love them because they are accurate, exquisitely crafted, and, of course, expensive as any fine *objet d'art*. For the same reasons target shooters love these rifles, criminals ignore them. In fact, gun-control advocates cannot name a single crime in which .50-caliber rifles have been used.

That has not kept the Violence Policy Center from working with liberal senators to give the BATF the authority to "regulate the design, manufacture, and distribution of firearms and ammunition" and to "ban certain models or classes of weapons." Senator Dianne Feinstein has proposed a "Military Sniper Weapon Regulation Act" that would ultimately require all ".50-caliber" owners to forfeit their rifles. She makes no distinction between the gun owner's .50 round and other calibers in the .50 range.

Take note. In her legislation, we can see the birth of a soundbite from the Buzzword Factory, as "assault weapons" are joined by "sniper weapons."

"Saturday Night Specials":
Discriminating by Paycheck, Class, and Color

> I can remember the days when we could get a call and be there in three or four minutes. We don't have that today. I've called the police myself and waited an hour.
> —*Will Craig Roberts, Master Officer, Tulsa*

Those who've been pushing a ban on so-called Saturday night specials over the years want us to believe that low-income people (and let's be honest, the stereotype we're being guided toward here involves mostly minorities) head to the neighborhood gun store at, say, 5 P.M. on a Saturday. They buy their cheap guns, head to the liquor store for some malt liquor, and then settle in for a nice evening of cards, pool, and a little bullet-dodging.

That image plays on a stereotype gun-control proponents want to exploit to get us to ban inexpensive, small-caliber, compact handguns for low-income people. Again, the facts are decidedly inconvenient.

• *Most handguns are "Saturday night specials."* The U.S. Treasury Department and BATF reported to Congress, "Self-defense handguns are generally small, lightweight revolvers and semiautomatic pistols, varying from .22 to .38 caliber."[42]

• *The law-abiding poor are most at risk.* The violent crime victimization rate is highest among people with annual incomes below $7,500.[43]

• *Inexpensive handguns contribute mightily to the 2.5 million times a year a crime is avoided.* The Justice Department found that 34 percent of felons have been scared off, shot at, wounded, or captured by an armed citizen, and that 40 percent have not committed crimes because they feared that their potential victims were armed. That's the lifesaving efficacy of affordable handguns.[44]

• *"Saturday night specials" are* not *preferred by criminals.* "SNSs are involved in only about 1–3 percent of all violent crimes," writes criminologist Gary Kleck. "Most handgun criminals do not use SNSs, and most SNSs are not owned or used for criminal purposes. Instead, most are probably owned by poor people for protection."[45] Justice Department studies have found that "There is no evidence to suggest that criminals prefer smaller *caliber* guns...or cheaper weapons," and "the often-assumed criminal preference for small, cheap handguns is not confirmed."[46]

A Civil Rights Issue

Compact guns go back to the beginning of the Republic. Thomas Jefferson, George Mason, and other eighteenth-century statesmen carried small pistols. By 1877, it was estimated that one Chicagoan out of ten carried a concealed pistol.

While compact pistols are something of an American tradition, so too, unfortunately, are efforts to disarm African-Americans.

In its infamous decision upholding slavery, *Dred Scott* v. *Sanford*, the U.S. Supreme Court viewed with horror the prospect that citizenship "would give to persons of the Negro race, who were recognized as citizens in any one State of the Union, the right to enter every other State whenever they pleased...and it would give them the full liberty of speech in public and in private upon all subjects upon which its own citizens might speak; to hold public meetings upon political affairs, and to keep and carry arms wherever they went."

Dred Scott was a despicable opinion that upheld slavery. But it did get one thing right. It equated the rights of free speech and assembly with the right to keep and bear arms.[47]

Following the Civil War, into the era of civil rights, racists of various sorts have also paid perverse respect to this principle by trying to restrict the Second Amendment rights of African-Americans.

Evidence clearly indicates that the belief that so-called "Saturday Night Specials" are used to commit the great majority of felonies is misleading and counterproductive.

–Police Foundation, Firearm Abuse, 1977

The infamous Jim Crow era forbade African-Americans in many states from owning guns. Consider Tennessee's "Army and Navy" law of 1879, which prohibited the sale of any "belt or pocket pistols, or revolvers, or any other kinds of pistols, except Army or Navy pistol" models—in short, the law prohibited the sale of the least expensive handguns of that time. Sound familiar? The intended effect, of course, was to deny African-Americans the very guns they could afford just as the Klan was getting organized. A U.S. senator from Tennessee worked hard to pass a national version of this forerunner of the Saturday night special law.

Of the Gun Control Act of 1968, *anti*gun journalist Robert Sherrill wrote that it "was passed not to control guns but to control blacks.... Inasmuch as the legislation finally passed in 1968 had nothing to do with the guns used in the assassinations of King and Robert Kennedy, it seems reasonable to assume that the law was directed at that other threat of the 1960s, more omnipresent than the political assassin—namely, the black rioter.... With the horrendous rioting of 1967 and 1968, Congress again was panicked toward passing some law that would shut off weapons access to blacks."[48]

In the 1990s, low-income minorities saw their right to arms further encroached upon by public housing authorities, backed by a Clinton administration eager to prohibit firearms. It deserves to be said that modern attempts against "Saturday night specials" would violate the Constitution's Equal Protection clause by having a "disproportionate impact on poor people."

The first time many people hear this argument, they may be taken aback. They may regard the idea of gun ownership as a civil rights issue to be a strained blending of concerns. If it strikes you this way, remember that our civil rights are those expressed and codified by our Bill of Rights. Whatever your race, religion, or background, if anyone denies your right to a firearm, make no mistake—they have violated your Second Amendment right, one of your most basic civil rights.

A Women's Issue

Compact handguns are popular for concealed carry because of their thinner grips. This and their shorter distance between grips and triggers make them ideal for people with small hands. Hence compact handguns are ideal for women, as well as for many elderly people. What some call "Saturday night specials" we call tools of personal protection for the most vulnerable.

You could obtain a compact handgun if you feel you need it to be safe. Or you could do what spokesmen for gun controllers Jim and Sarah Brady have advised. If someone breaks into your home, they say, "Put up no defense—give them what they want."[49]

But what do you do if what they want is *you*?

Solution: Enforce the (20,000) Laws We Already Have on the Books

Currently there are more than 20,000 firearms laws in the United States, including those imposed by the National Firearms Act (1934), the Gun Control Act (1968), and the Firearms Owners' Protection Act (1986), among others, as well as restrictions imposed by most states and many localities.

• It is a crime punishable with ten years' imprisonment for anyone to alter a semi-automatic firearm to make it fire fully automatically.

• It is a crime punishable with ten years' imprisonment for anyone to possess such an altered firearm.

• It is a crime punishable with ten years' imprisonment for anyone to trade or sell such an altered firearm.

• It is a crime punishable with ten years' imprisonment for a convicted felon to possess any firearm.

• The use of a firearm in a violent or drug-trafficking crime is punishable by a five-year mandatory prison sentence. A second conviction brings a twenty-year mandatory sentence or life imprisonment without parole if the firearm is a machine gun or is equipped with a silencer.

• It is a crime punishable by a mandatory fifteen years' imprisonment for a criminal with three prior violent or drug-related felonies to possess any firearm.

• It is a crime punishable with ten years' imprisonment to transfer a firearm knowing that it will be used to commit a violent or drug-trafficking crime.

• It is a crime punishable with ten years' imprisonment to transport or receive firearms or ammunition in interstate commerce with intent to commit a felony.

• It is a crime punishable with ten years' imprisonment to shorten the barrel(s) of a shotgun to less than eighteen inches or a rifle to less than sixteen inches.

• It is a crime punishable with ten years' imprisonment to travel from one state to another and acquire, or attempt to acquire, a firearm with the intent to use it in a violent felony.

• It is a crime punishable with ten years' imprisonment to alter the serial number of a firearm.

• It is a crime punishable with ten years' imprisonment to possess a firearm with an altered serial number.

• If more than one such firearm is involved, the criminal faces imprisonment for the same number of years for each gun. In addition to imprisonment, fines for violating federal firearms laws can be as high as $250,000. That's federal law now.

We have plenty of gun laws. However, the gun-control elites in Washington have no interest in seeing them enforced.[50]

Verbal Firestorm

Wayne LaPierre, of the NRA, let me start with you. You created quite a firestorm last week with this comment. Let me put it on the screen for you and our viewers.

Wayne LaPierre: "I've come to believe, he, President Clinton, needs a certain level of violence in this country. He's willing to accept a certain level of killing to further his political agenda and the vice president too."

—*Tim Russert, NBC's* Meet the Press

This was strong language. But the facts lead inexorably to this interpretation.

Consider this: While the last administration worked hard to concoct new reasons for more gun-control laws, federal enforcement of existing federal gun laws against criminals declined by 50 percent.

When then attorney general Janet Reno appeared before the Senate Judiciary Committee, she was challenged to defend the horrible, shameful rate of prosecutions. Asked if any improvements could be made, she shook her head and said, "No." Apparently, she regarded gun criminals as "guppies," small fry.[51]

When federal prosecutors started Project Exile in Richmond, Virginia, the program that rounded up violent felons convicted for gun violations, murder by guns fell 65 percent in that city. You would think success on such a scale would be rewarded and emulated. To their astonishment, far from getting kudos from Washington, the prosecutors found themselves frozen out by their Justice Department colleagues. The Clinton administration also refused to take

Project Exile nationwide. Money to expand the program was squeezed off. The Clinton people rewrote the rules so that a criminal had to have up to three or more felony convictions before he could be brought in for a firearms violation.[52]

Even less excusable was the way that the most pro–gun control administration in history walked away from its responsibility to make the instant background checks and other systems work to keep guns out of the hands of criminals.

We mentioned earlier in this chapter how, despite a $300 million investment, the federal government was unable or unwilling to get its instant check to the same standard as your gasoline credit card.

Another sign of the gun controllers' lack of honest interest in gun crime can be seen in the slim number of referrals made by the BATF, numbers that declined sharply in the last administration. A study by the Transactional Records Access Clearinghouse at Syracuse University (TRAC), which analyzes law-enforcement data, reported that BATF gun referrals to federal prosecutors had dropped by 44 percent from 1992 to 1999. In all, the agency charged with enforcing federal firearms referred 5,510 cases to federal prosecutors in 1998. There had also been a matching decline in the number of prosecutions. About half of those actually were prosecuted.[53]

Breaking these numbers down by city, the BATF referred a grand total of *16* cases in Washington, D.C.—easily the most murderous city in America—to prosecutors in 1998. Chicago had 45 referrals that year, and San Francisco had 29. Richmond, Virginia, home to Project Exile, had 326.[54]

An interesting conclusion could be drawn from these examples. In places with heavy gun-control laws, there is little pressure to crack down on criminals. In places where citizens are allowed to own guns, law enforcement invests its resources against crime.

Imagine if the BATF were to refer just ten cases a month to every one of the one hundred U.S. attorneys in the nation; we would take twelve thousand violent felons off the streets of the United States. Better yet, bring it up to twenty, and we'd remove twenty-four thousand.

At this writing, the Bush administration is just beginning to grapple with the need to put some muscle behind laws that crack down on gun-toting criminals. Removing those twenty-four thousand violent felons would go a long way in restoring safe streets.

We should make the most of successful programs like Project Exile, Project Safe Neighborhoods, and Project CUFF (Criminal Use of Firearms by Felons), which prosecutes in federal court criminals caught with a firearm. Implemented in Mobile, Alabama, by U.S. attorney Jeff Sessions, CUFF was a runaway success. Now a U.S. senator, Sessions says, "It is time to stop talking about political programs that will not reduce crimes committed with firearms, and start implementing practical programs that will. The safety of our children is too important to do otherwise."[55]

Fortunately, we have a U.S. President who gets it. President Bush is moving forward on national action on gun crime. In summer 2002, Attorney General John Ashcroft launched Project Safe Neighborhoods, a $533 million, two-year national offensive against gun criminals. The Bush Justice Department will fund 580 state and local prosecutors dedicated to processing gun violence cases. They will be backstopped by 94 new assistant U.S. attorneys dedicated to violent gun crime.[56]

Not everyone gets it, however. Instead of enforcing the law, or fixing NICS, gun-control politicians are waging a new campaign to turn instant check into a permanent, national gun registry. The false rationale cited by gun controllers, once again, is terrorism. Attorney General John Ashcroft stood tough, refusing to be intimidated by calls to keep the records of law-abiding citizens who cleared their check.

There is, however, little room for law-abiding gun owners to relax. Under Janet Reno, the Justice Department kept these NICS records in an "audit log" for six months. Attorney General Ashcroft reduced that to no more than twenty-four hours—a huge step in the right direction. But now Senators Ted Kennedy and Chuck Schumer are piggybacking on terrorism to try to make this practice permanent. They want to make your NICS record of cleared purchases available to "any federal, state or local law enforcement agency in connection with a civil or criminal law enforcement investigation."

Second Amendment advocates must be particularly vigilant. Current law requires that all such records of *cleared purchases* be destroyed. We have seen where creating such a national registry has led in Canada, Australia, and Great Britain.

The Second Amendment Today

A well-regulated Militia, being necessary to the security of a free State, the right of the people to keep and bear Arms, shall not be infringed.   *—United States Constitution*

When Patrick Henry said, "The great object is, that every man be armed," he was addressing more than the needs of a rural, agrarian society. He offered, as the Founders always did, a vision of a better society for all people, for all time. Richard Henry Lee meant the same when he wrote, "To preserve liberty it is essential that the whole body of the people always possess arms."

Always.

In Chapter Five, we'll examine the history of the Second Amendment, the intention of the Founders, and how a dishonest generation of "revisionist" scholars have tried to revise history out of existence (to the point, in one notorious case, of actually fabricating facts).

The point here is that your right to keep and bear arms is under assault *today*, from multiple angles, by a large and tireless collection of pressure groups. Many have intentions that are as honorable as they are naive, but their instinct, as with the recent curtailment of the First Amendment by the "campaign finance reform" law, is always to move in degrees to make us a less free society. They do this because they do not trust the common man, the common woman, to act wisely. They place all their trust *not* in personal responsibility, but in the kind of top-down authority our Founders despised. They have lost their connection with the American Founders, and in some significant ways, what it means to be an American.

In the name of political correctness, they make sure that airport security is as universal and ineffective as possible. So we see the red-faced, teary-eyed women singled out, grandmothers shaken down, grandfathers who fought for their country in various stages of undress, even pilots themselves treated like suspects. We have a government aching to implement a national ID card, whether from state driver's licenses, retinal scans, voiceprint, hand geometry, or DNA—it doesn't matter. We have a federal government that often seems more interested in tracking us than in tracking the terrorists.

What the Founders wished to reinforce for all time with their Second Amendment was that the right to keep and bear arms was a matter not just of utility, but of freedom and human dignity.

It was—and is—a way of ensuring respect for home, for property, for person.

But more than that, the recognized right to defend oneself is an essential part of the Founders' Enlightenment vision of what the whole man, the whole woman, could be. It was as basic to their concept of freedom as anything in the U.S. Constitution.

That is why the Founders gave this amendment second place, pairing it forever with the First Amendment, our right to free speech.

That is our birthright. That is our heritage. That is what is at stake.

Chapter Three

Citizen Rights
The Proven Way to Combat Crime

...the Second Amendment does not merely protect sport shooting and hunting, though it certainly does that.

Nor does the Second Amendment exist to protect the government's right to bear arms.

The framers of our Constitution wrote the Second Amendment with a greater purpose.

They made the Second Amendment the law of the land because it has something very particular to say about the rights of every man and every woman, and about the relationship of every man and every woman to his or her Government.

That is: The first right of every human being, the right of self-defense.

—Senator Larry Craig

The year was 1991, five years before Texas enacted a right-to-carry law that allowed most Texas citizens to carry concealed weapons. Seventy-one-year-old Al Gratia had just sat down to lunch at Luby's cafeteria in Killeen, Texas, with his wife, Ursula "Suzy" Kunath Gratia, sixty-seven, and daughter, Dr. Suzanna Gratia, then thirty-two.

Minutes later, while daughter and parents were enjoying their time together, a blue Ford pickup truck shattered the restaurant's plate-glass window. George Hennard of nearby Belton, Texas—a rangy, muscle-bound man of thirty-five—stepped out onto the broken glass and methodically began to work his way around the room with two pistols, pumping bullets into one diner after another.

"This is what Belton did to me," he screamed. "Was it worth it?"

Dr. Gratia tried to restrain her father, a veteran of World War II, from getting up from behind their table. "I have to do something," Al said.

"It was very frustrating for him to be a sitting duck," she would later recall. Her effort did not succeed. Al Gratia did "do something." He lunged toward the murderer, only to be shot in the chest and fall to the ground, dying. At that moment, a restaurant patron broke out a window, and the panicked customers and cafeteria employees began to flee for safety. Dr. Gratia tried to pull her mother along.

"She wouldn't go," she said. Ursula walked to her husband of forty-seven years, and knelt over him, becoming Hennard's next victim. In all, twenty-three people were killed in Luby's that day.[1]

Now a Texas state legislator, Representative Suzanna Gratia-Hupp remembers "how angry I felt just waiting for this man to get to me next." She was angry, too, that in Texas at that time the law required her to leave her gun in her car. In those days, she said, you had "no way of defending yourself against this crazy man with a gun." If she had been armed, "there's no doubt in my mind that I could have saved my parents and at least twelve to thirteen others."

• • •

Thomas Terry walked into a Shoney's restaurant in Anniston, Alabama, expecting nothing more than a quick meal. Instead, he found himself face-to-face with two armed robbers, crazed gunmen who had terrorized the other restaurant patrons, and were working themselves into a frenzy, on the verge of an orgy of violence. Only then did Terry pull the concealed .45-caliber handgun Alabama law allowed him to carry.

The thugs fired, one of them grazing Terry's hip. Terry's aim was more sure.

He shot one of the armed robbers to death, and wounded the other to a degree that took him out of the fight.[2]

• • •

Two cases from the previous decade, two different outcomes. One involved a citizen who could be legally armed. One did not. Both illustrate the insanity of restricting law-abiding citizens, while gun-toting maniacs and criminals operate freely.

How easy is it for violent criminals to get guns? A few years ago, at an NRA rally in Washington, D.C., a young man walked up to one of the rally leaders. With a slight, ironic smile he said: "I'm one of those criminals you're talking about. When people talk about not selling me guns, I say, 'Are you kidding?' I can get a gun in ten minutes. I live in a halfway house down the street. Whenever I get in the mood, I'm gonna start robbing people in ten minutes."[3]

He laughed and started to walk away.

"Got to eat, man."

In a city like Richmond where prosecutors go after gun-toting violent felons, that young man would be eating from a prison lunch tray. In Washington, D.C., he is apt to have *you* for lunch. But he was right about one thing. While red tape fouls up law-abiding citizens, criminals never enter into the red tape zone.

Consider the case of Jamil Abdullah Al-Amin, known to millions as H. Rap Brown, famous for saying in the 1960s that violence is "as American as cherry pie." The five-year sentence he served for his role in a robbery and shootout should have made it impossible for Brown to have owned a gun. Nevertheless, when two deputies in Atlanta came by to serve the fifty-eight-year-old man with a warrant on relatively minor charges, they found an ex-con armed to the teeth. He wounded both deputies, and followed up by firing into their prone bodies.

Deputy Ricky Kinchen died. Deputy Aldranon English survived to identify Brown—who was later apprehended in Alabama with the very same two guns he should never have been allowed to buy.[4] Several years before, Brown had been caught breaking a number of federal gun laws. In fact, a local prosecutor had asked the federal government to prosecute, but the Justice Department had declined.[5]

Or consider the story of another gun-toting felon in the Midwest named Ben Smith. Smith was an advocate of white racism instead of "black power," but his case bore powerful resemblances to Brown's. He, too, was a convicted criminal who was able to obtain a gun from the black market.[6] Smith had previously tried to buy a gun at a store in Illinois, but had been refused because of his criminal record. The attempt to purchase was a federal crime in and of itself, but no one followed up, not the state or the feds. Had they done so, they might have kept Smith from a rampage of hate.

Smith wound up on a Friday night in July at West Rodgers Park, a place where Orthodox Jewish men and women and their children routinely walk to Sabbath service on Friday nights, and launched a night of terror. He opened fire, shooting five adults and a child. He then went to nearby Skokie to shoot and kill Ricky Birdsong, a former basketball coach at Northwestern University, who was out for an evening walk with his children. Several days later, Smith wound up in Bloomington, Indiana, where he killed a Korean man before killing himself.

Each of these stories provoked media outrage over the availability of guns. And in each case, when you scratch below the surface, you see that the untold story is how many murders would be prevented if

• the government executed the law and went after violent felons who possess guns or who attempt to obtain them.

• ordinary, law-abiding people could be armed and able to fight back.

Of course, gun-control advocates will tell you that there is always another option. You could depend on the police.

This is what eighty-three-year-old James Edward Scott was forced to do by Baltimore police after he shot and wounded one of the burglars who repeatedly harassed him and invaded his West Baltimore property. Criminologist John Lott tells how the police made Scott dependent on them by taking away his .22-caliber rifle. When the next intruder broke into Scott's house, however, the police were nowhere to be seen. They were not there to keep him from being strangled to death.

In this and so many cases, the police cannot be everywhere at once. They cannot always protect you. They certainly cannot be your personal bodyguards. You can, however, count on them to show up to investigate your crime scene and draw chalk marks around your body.[7]

Every time. Eventually.

Lott notes the story of Mr. Scott, and adds several other cases of endangered citizens being disarmed by the police, including the infamous case of Alan Berg, the "liberal Denver talk-show host who took great delight in provoking and insulting those with whom he disagreed. Berg attempted to obtain a permit after receiving death threats from white supremacists, but the police first attempted to talk him out of applying and then ultimately rejected his request. Shortly after he was denied, Berg was murdered by members of the Aryan Nation."[8]

For the most part, the police are dedicated to living up to the motto many have on the side of their cars, "To Serve and Protect." But if you count on them being there when you need them, you are gambling with your life.

Ohio: 911 Tape Transcript
"Police Department."
"A man is trying to break in my door. . . . I don't know who he is. He's at my home."
"He's doing what?"

"He's trying to break in my door."

"...what's your name, ma'am?"

"Sharon."

"Sharon? I want you to stay on the telephone, okay?"

"Okay."

"Where are you now?"

"I locked the front door and I'm upstairs in the bedroom."

"Is there anyone with you?"

"No, just my baby."

"Sharon, are you still there?"

"[Screaming] He's in the house! He's broke through the door."

"He broke in. Sharon, are you still there?"

"Uh-huh."

"Shut the bedroom door, lock it if you can, and come right back to the phone."

"HE'S AT THE DOOR!"

"What?"

"He's at the door!!! He's here!! HE'S HERE!!"

"Are you still with me? Tell him you've got the police on the phone."

"I've got the police on the phone. Who are you? Why are you here?"

"He's in the bedroom with her."

"I've got the police on the phone. I've got the police on the phone.... Why are you here? Why are you here? Why? Why?" Sharon's voice breaks into sobs. She begins screaming.

"Sharon? Sharon?"

A hand slams down the receiver. Dial tone.

Sharon was raped.

She became a statistic because the criminal in her bedroom wagered—correctly—that he could victimize her long before the police could arrive.

Police response time was one of the prime reasons Floridians passed a right-to-carry law. Back in the mid-1980s, in some parts of the state it was taking up to two hours to get a harried and over-whelmed police force to respond to a call. Columnist George F. Will put the citizens' dilemma in the form of a mordant challenge—call the police, call for an ambulance, call for a pizza, and see which one arrives first.

The truth is, in most crimes, there will only be two people present, a perpetrator and a victim. Most of the time everyone else shows up later. Though the police may be dedicated to responding to your call as fast as they can humanly manage (against other, equally urgent calls), it is important to remember one other key fact: *The police are not legally bound to come to your aid.*

In a 1981 ruling, the D.C. Court of Appeals found that "a government and its agents are under no general duty to provide public services, such as police protection, to any particular citizen."[9] Little wonder that spending on private security doubled from 1980 to 1996, with the percentage of gun ownership among adults rising from 26 percent to almost 40 percent.[10]

This trend toward citizen self-protection is born of necessity, when people make realistic assessments of their vulnerability. Your ability to protect yourself, however, is a fundamental right that many would take away.

For example, the Violence Policy Center—which openly supports a total ban on handguns—advocates subjecting firearms to "consumer safety" regulations enforced by the BATF. The reason for this regulation, one spokesman said on a national radio show, is because "we believe that ultimately handguns would be phased out through such an agency."[11]

According to Sarah Brady, spiritual leader of the gun-control movement, "the only reason for guns in civilian hands is for sporting purposes."[12] Another prominent gun controller at the Brady Center Legal Action Project said that self-defense is not a "federally guaranteed constitutional right."[13]

In fact, when the Brady Campaign people—the gun-ban advocates formerly known as Handgun Control, Inc.—issue report cards ranking the quality of state laws over five-year stretches, they give an "F" to states like Kentucky, Louisiana, Maine, Montana, and Wyoming, where gun ownership is prevalent, while giving the state of Maryland an "A." It does not seem to bother anyone at the Brady Campaign that Maryland's average violent crime rate is double the average rate for the five "F" states.[14]

The point is clear. Crime is irrelevant to the gun-control community. Control is the issue.

Federal City Blues

Remember the shooting at the National Zoo in Washington, D.C., that prompted then vice president Al Gore to take a stand for gun locks?

It was African-American Family Celebration Day at the National Zoo on a pleasant Easter Monday. The ominous tone of the day was set by several fights that had broken out among rival groups of teenagers. About 6 P.M., as people were filing out of the gates of the zoo onto Connecticut Avenue, groups of teens began throwing bottles at one another. The fight escalated, and shots rang out. Seven children were struck and one, Harris Bates, eleven, was wounded critically.

The next day, the Washington police arrested sixteen-year-old Antoine Bernard Jones and charged him with the shooting. Jones was well known to the police. He had an extensive juvenile record, including an armed robbery when he was thirteen. Jones had been expelled and suspended from school for making death threats. His father, James Antonio Jones, in prison at that time, was an enforcer for a major Washington drug lord who ruled the District's cocaine trade.

Several witnesses told police they had seen the younger Jones flashing and brandishing a 9mm pistol inside the zoo earlier in the day. Several had also fingered Jones as the shooter.[15]

The National Zoo shooting sent the gun-control mob into near hysterics. The Million Mom March used the incident in its advertising to promote the event on the National Mall. Liberal pundits clucked their tongues and cited the tragedy as further evidence of the need for even more restrictions on gun rights. Yet amid all the hype, hoopla, hand-wringing, and histrionics, the truth did manage to seep out. In fact, the public reaction stunned smugly self-righteous gun controllers. The shooting at the National Zoo was widely seen as proof of exactly the opposite of what gun controllers were loudly claiming. It was seen by a skeptical public as powerful evidence of the complete failure of gun control.

Why? Because everything Antoine Jones did at the zoo that day already was illegal in Washington, D.C. If ever there was a laboratory for the testing of gun-control myths, it has been the nation's capital.

The fact is, Jones had already broken scores of laws when he slipped a 9mm into his pants pocket and headed for the zoo. After all, that was already a criminal act in Washington, where all ownership and possession of handguns was banned in 1975. Possessing a handgun as a juvenile was against the law. And shooting indiscriminately into a group of innocent people is a crime everywhere.

The gun controllers were quick to counter with the well-worn argument that Washington's high gun-crime rate is due to the ready availability of guns. The culprits, we are told, are the neighboring states of Maryland and especially gun-friendly Virginia. The District's congressional delegate, Eleanor Holmes Norton, exploited the zoo shooting to call for a national gun ban so that states with restrictive firearms laws would not be "flooded" with guns from states with weaker statutes. Mayor Anthony Williams of Washington demanded a nationwide ban on handgun ownership (to make, in effect, all of America into a larger version of Washington, D.C.). Vice President Al Gore, then running for president, pounced on the National Zoo shooting as a pretext to push for national gun laws. President Clinton predictably weighed in at several party fund-raisers, citing the zoo shooting as evidence of the need for more gun control.

Yet the public understood that if all the laws already on the books could not stop Antoine Jones from shooting up the National Zoo, then how would passing more laws do anything? In a city in which all gun ownership was effectively banned, what was left to do?

Antoine Jones may have stolen the 9mm he used at the zoo. He may have bought it illegally on the street or borrowed it from a criminal associate. But he did not buy it legally in either Virginia or Maryland, the alleged source of the guns that cause so much crime in Washington, D.C. In Virginia, no one younger than eighteen can legally hold, possess, or transport a handgun, with certain exceptions. It is also unlawful for anyone under age twenty-nine with a juvenile conviction, which Jones had, to possess or transport a handgun. In Maryland, no one under eighteen can possess, a handgun and no one convicted of a crime as a juvenile can own or possess a handgun.

Moreover, if Virginia was the source of Washington's illegal gun culture, as the gun-control crowd claims, shouldn't Virginia have even worse problems with gun-related crime? Yet, passing across Memorial Bridge from Washington, D.C., into Virginia's Arlington County, you enter a zone in which the level of crime is fifty times lower.

Nor can Washington's political and opinion elite argue that all they need is more time for the law to work. The groundwork for Washington's experiment had been set at the height of President Lyndon Johnson's "Great Society" when Congress passed the Gun Control Act of 1968.[16] How the citizens of the nation's capital wound up in a supposedly "gunless" society is a story that describes the piecemeal evolution of gun control in every democracy.

As with so many gun-control regimes, the restrictions began with an explicit promise in the 1968 federal law that it would not restrict "law-abiding citizens with respect to the acquisition, possession, or use of firearms appropriate to the purpose of hunting, trapshooting, target shooting, personal protection or any other lawful activity, and that this title *is not intended to discourage or eliminate the private ownership or use of firearms by law-abiding citizens for lawful purposes*" (emphasis added).

Undeterred by the clear intent of Congress expressed in the 1968 Act and eager to try out its pet theories, the District of Columbia Council in 1976 imposed the Firearms Control Regulations Act on the hapless citizens of the nation's capital. The act's sweeping measures prohibited possession of *any* handgun that was not registered with the police prior to September 24, 1976, and reregistered by February 5, 1977. The act also required the registration of all privately owned firearms and that all firearms kept at home be rendered inoperable, useless for self-defense or protection, by requiring them to be kept unloaded, disassembled, or bound by a gun lock or similar device. In short, keeping a loaded firearm of any kind inside one's own home became a crime in Washington.[17]

The politicians might as well have hung out signs: *"Attention burglars, rapists, drug dealers, thieves, and armed robbers: All law-abiding citizens in the District of Columbia have been disarmed. All homes and places of business in Washington have been mandated gun-free. Prey at will."*

The results of this experiment have been entirely predictable and catastrophic.

Prior to the total ban on gun ownership, the murder rate in Washington had been falling. As soon as the gun ban became law, the homicide rate began to rise, then soar. *Between 1977 and 1991, Washington's homicide rate tripled.*[18]

The gun controllers pooh-poohed these concerns and barged ahead with their precious experiment in social engineering. Their belief in gun control remained unshaken by mere facts and real-world experience. To paraphrase George Orwell, gun control is an idea that only an intellectual could believe.

In fact, many intellectuals who espoused gun control expressly did not believe in it. Consider the case of the late Carl Rowan, syndicated columnist, former ambassador to Finland. A resident of the D.C. upper-crust Northwest section, Rowan had a simple position on gun control, he was passionately in favor of it ... that is, until the summer evening in 1988 when he heard someone rattling around his bedroom window.

Rowan looked out at his backyard and saw four strangers bunched around his swimming pool and Jacuzzi. Rowan called the police, and retrieved—you guessed it—a .22-caliber handgun. He was about to unlock a gate to let in the police, when he suddenly found himself confronted by a large man, sopping wet in his underwear, the acrid smell of marijuana clinging to him.

The man approached Rowan.

"Stop. I have a gun," Rowan said.

The man kept coming.

Twice more Rowan warned the young man, but he kept coming until, the columnist later testified, "he lunged at me."

Rowan shot him in the wrist.

Despite this experience, Rowan continued to adamantly maintain a vehement pro–gun control position for Washington, D.C.[19]

Rowan's case had a relatively happy ending. Many times, the lack of Second Amendment protections in our nation's capital has resulted in tragedy. Around the time of the disappearance (and we know now, the murder) of Chandra Levy, a number of professional women disappeared, their bodies turning up later in rivers and parks. One can only wonder how many of these capital-city murder victims would be alive and with us today if they had been allowed to protect themselves.

We must reverse this psychology [of needing guns for home defense]. We can do it by passing a law that says anyone found in possession of a handgun except a legitimate officer of the law goes to jail—period!

—Carl Rowan, Washington, D.C., syndicated columnist, 1981

...as long as authorities leave this society awash in drugs and guns, I will protect my family.

—Carl Rowan, 1988

Chicago, A-Train to Ruin

In Chicago, as in Washington, D.C., and so many other parts of the world, registration preceded confiscation. Chicago's handgun registration requirement in 1968 had no effect on the city's rising handgun homicide numbers. After peaking in 1974, Chicago homicides declined until the 1980s. Nevertheless, in April 1982, Chicago's politicians felt the need to enact a law prohibiting possession of handguns not previously registered with the police. Annual handgun homicide numbers and percentages of total homicides fluctuated, then rose sharply. By the end of the 1990s, Chicago had the third highest homicide rate among major U.S. cities.

Many of Chicago's suburbs suffered the same experience. After suburban Evanston banned handguns in mid-1982, Evanston's robbery rate rose 8 percent the following year (while nationwide suburban areas experienced a 20 percent decline, and the U.S. rate declined 16 percent).

When the village of Oak Park banned handgun sales in 1977, rates of violent crime and burglary rose sharply. Like a nineteenth-century physician bleeding a patient, only to wonder why he continued to get worse, Oak Park responded to this problem with more "cure"— banning private possession of handguns altogether in 1984. The suburb continued to be plagued by crime. In 1986, Oak Park had the temerity to prosecute a local man who used a handgun to fire on robbers who held him up at his service station. Out of sympathy, the mayor of Kennesaw, Georgia, declared the Oak Park man to be an honorary citizen of Kennesaw, and presented him a plaque stating that the Georgia town was "proud of citizens such as yourself who stand up for their constitutional rights to own and bear arms in defense of their lives and property." When challenged by a reporter about Oak Park's increase in burglaries after banning possession of handguns, the village's president could only accuse the journalist of trying to "insist on the gun nut being right."

States of Denial

Many states have moved in the direction of Washington, D.C., and Chicago, attempting to reduce crime with gun control, only to repeat their same results—more crime.

• California increased its waiting period on retail and private sales of handguns from five to fifteen days in 1975 (reduced to ten days in 1996). It outlawed eleven "assault weapons" in 1989. It subjected rifles and shotguns to a waiting period in 1990. *Yet since 1975, the state's annual homicide rate has averaged 34 percent higher than the rate for the rest of the country.*

• Maryland imposed a waiting period and a gun purchase limit, banned several small handguns, restricted "assault weapons," and regulated private transfers of firearms even between family members and friends. *Yet its homicide rate is 59 percent higher than the rate for the rest of the country.*

In fact, the overall homicide rate in the jurisdictions that have the most severe restrictions on firearms purchases and ownership—California, Illinois, Maryland, New Jersey, New York, and Washington, D.C.—is 23 percent higher than the rate for the rest of the country.

And when crime gets worse in these gun-control states, what do the politicians do? Bleed the patient some more!

The (Real) Police Story

During the Clinton administration, we saw time after time the president appear before the cameras to make sweeping gun-control proposals in front of a phalanx of blue uniforms. The impression was that America's law-enforcement community stands foursquare behind gun control.

Like so many "facts" from this era, police support for gun control was the product of political spin and the clever stage mastery of Mr. Clinton's "advance teams."

The trend by the rank-and-file police officer to publicly oppose gun-control legislation has been growing for several years.

—Ken Zigler, Baltimore Fraternal Order of Police

To be fair, gun control does have high-profile proponents in the law-enforcement community. Yet many of these backers of gun control are senior-ranking officers in cities where advocating the politically correct opinions of liberal mayors and city councils is a smart career move. When you look at a broader picture, the real position of American law enforcement looks more like, well, broader American opinion.

While some officers were lining up behind Clinton and Gore at gun-control venues in the mid-1990s, other officers testified to Congress about their very different views. Lieutenant Dennis Tueller of Salt Lake City reported the collected results of national police polls. He reported that

- 96.4 percent of officers support private ownership of firearms for self-protection;[20]
- 95 percent oppose the ban on large-capacity magazines;
- 92 percent do not support the so-called "assault weapons" ban;
- 93 percent disagree with the Brady Act;
- 84.6 percent believe gun control does not lessen crime.[21]

Tens of thousands of law-enforcement officers are members of the National Rifle Association because they have lived one of the lessons of our times—that even the most dedicated police officers cannot protect every potential victim. They understand, as most Americans do, that public safety is the public's business.

Getting Tough

For officers on the street, debates over gun issues are more than political exercises. Every year, hundreds of police officers lose their lives to gun violence. They have a greater incentive than anyone to see no guns in the hands of violent criminals.

And so they have more reason than anyone to be outraged by the government's sorry record on gun-crime investigations and prosecutions. In 1998, to take one recent year as a representative sample, federal referrals for prosecutions for gun crimes numbered

- eight cases for the possession or discharge of firearms on school grounds;

- eight cases for the transfer of handgun ammunition to a juvenile;

- one referral to prosecutors resulting from a criminal attempting to buy guns, turned up by a Brady Act background check.[22]

Imagine that: Hundreds of millions of dollars spent on background checks, and only one referral of one criminal attempting to buy guns he shouldn't have.

The police understand that we don't need new gun laws. They understand—all too well—how much safer the streets would be if the federal government and prosecutors went all out to keep guns out of the hands of violent criminals.

With their safety, and ours, in mind, we could take a few steps to make America safe from gun violence:

1. Make programs that track and prosecute convicted violent felons with guns, like Richmond's Project Exile, a feature in every major city.

2. Support mandatory hard time for criminals who commit gun crimes.

3. Support legislation, like the widely popular "three strikes and you're out" law, that sends career criminals to finish their careers in prison—as well as other get-tough measures, like truth in sentencing and the abolition or restriction of parole.

If America would undertake this simple three step process, we could stem the tide of criminal violence in America. Only one other step would then be needed—universal recognition of the inherent safety of allowing the law-abiding to carry concealed guns.

The Right-to-Carry Success Story

In Canada and Britain, both with tough gun-control laws, almost half of all burglaries are "hot burglaries" [when residents are home]. In contrast, the United States, with fewer restrictions, has a "hot burglary" rate of only 13 percent. Criminals are not just behaving differently by accident. Convicted American felons reveal in surveys that they are much more worried about armed victims than about running into the police.

—*John R. Lott, Jr.*, More Guns, Less Crime

Right-to-carry began as the ultimate outsider issue. But it soon became the commonsense idea that took over two-thirds of the United States. The concept, simple, powerful, revolutionary, came down to this: Why not allow law-abiding citizens with good records not only to own guns, but to carry them? In fact, why not allow them to carry them in a concealed manner? This would mean that a criminal could not be sure which potential victim was "packing." Wouldn't that uncertainty spread out the deterrent effect, offering a greater measure of protection to all, including the vast majority of people who elect not to carry guns?

Before 1987, only seven states had "shall issue" laws—meaning that firearm carrying permits had to be given to applicants who met certain reasonable standards (such as age twenty-one, clean record).

Then the right-to-carry debate came to Florida, one of the most populous states in the nation. Past NRA president Marion P. Hammer spearheaded the lobbying charge in her home state, where she also serves as the executive director of Unified Sportsmen of Florida.

When the Florida legislature considered a "shall issue" RTC law-in 1980, the measure drew support from a wide spectrum of law-enforcement organizations (including the Florida Sheriffs Association and the Florida Police Chiefs Association). It also elicited the predictable hysteria from the gun-control lobby.

There would be, Floridians were warned, a "Wild West" atmosphere in which traffic arguments would turn into deadly shootouts. Florida's cities—humid, hot, and packed with gun-toting people—would become the scene of urban bloodbaths. Florida, it was predicted, would become known as the "Gunshine State."

One newspaper opined: "[A] pistol-packing citizenry will mean itchier trigger fingers. South Florida's climate of smoldering fear would flash like napalm when every stranger totes a piece, and every mental snap in traffic could lead to the crack of gunfire."

Some may have underestimated Hammer, a diminutive grandmother. If they did, they got a quick lesson in respect. Hammer, who had become a crack shot as a South Carolina farm girl, loves competition—whether it is competitive target shooting at the range or competitive sparring with gun-control lobbyists in the halls of the legislature. Thanks to her tireless leadership, the bill was signed into law. Gun controllers waited for the carnage and the "I told you so's." Funny thing, though. The "I told you so's" went to the other side in that debate.

In its first five years, at a time when the U.S. homicide rate rose 9 percent, Florida's homicide rate fell by 23 percent. Only one-fifth of 1 percent of the licensees had their permits revoked. "When you compare that to the number of licenses that were issued, that's very small," marveled the director of the state licensing division. He added there had been "no record of any accidents or incidents from a lack of training," and that "Florida's concealed weapon law has been very successful."[23]

The law hardly turned Florida into the OK Corral East. "From a law enforcement perspective," wrote the head of the state law-enforcement commission to the governor, "the licensing process has not resulted in problems in the community from people arming themselves with concealed weapons."[24]

Those who stepped back and looked at the overall picture saw an even more amazing trend. For decades, the rate of growth in violent crime in Florida had outpaced that of the nation. After the law took effect, Florida's rate of violent crime declined *below* the national average.

Florida had flipped from being a state that led the trend *toward* violent crime, to being a state that led the trend *away* from violent crime.

With the example of Florida's policy success, the right-to-carry battle moved from small states with agrarian traditions to the big, urban mega-states. The next major right-to-carry battle would be fought in Texas—another mega-state, galvanized into action by the angry testimony of Dr. Suzanna Gratia-Hupp on the Luby's shooting that took her parents' lives. Texas at that time had a governor, one George W. Bush, who listened to her and vowed to make the Lone Star State a "safer place."

Once again, the hysteria lobby went into full gear. With right-to-carry, Texas would revert to some distant frontier past, where an accidental bumping of shoulders could precipitate a squaring-off, and then—"Draw, stranger."

The law took effect in 1996. Within four years, more than 215,000 Texans became active carriers of firearms. And within that period, 99.5 percent of them remained in good standing. Again, only a tiny fraction of a percent had their permits revoked, generally because of misdemeanor violations that had nothing to do with firearms.

All the horror stories I thought would come to pass didn't happen. . . . I think it's worked out well, and that says good things about the citizens who have permits. I'm a convert.

−Glen White, President, Dallas Police Association

And once again, the rate of violent crime plunged. As a result of right-to-carry (and tough new laws, like Texas Exile, that cracked down on criminals with guns), Texas did in fact become a safer place. State homicide rates fell precipitously—by 60 percent—from the rate under the previous governor, Ann Richards. Texas's homicide rate has declined to its lowest point since the 1950s. Murder rates in Texas fell by 25 percent between 1995 and 1997, much faster than the 16 percent decline in states without "shall-issue" laws. The incidence of rape fell twice as fast.[25]

The law-enforcement community stood by the candidate who embraced this commonsense solution. When he ran for president, George W. Bush received a strong endorsement from the Fraternal Order of Police and the 65,000-member Law Enforcement Alliance of America.

Now the successes of Florida and Texas are being duplicated in more than thirty other states. When they broke down the official data on crime and gun accidents, criminologists John R. Lott, Jr., and David B. Mustard found that in right-to-carry states

- murders fell by 8.5 percent;
- rapes and aggravated assaults fell by 5 percent and 7 percent, respectively.

If states without right-to-carry provisions had adopted them in 1992, in the next few years we could have prevented

- 1,570 murders;
- 4,177 rapes;
- more than 60,000 assaults;
- $6.214 billion in economic losses due to crime.[26]

Even criminals' lives were being saved. Criminologist Gary Kleck found that fewer than one in one thousand defensive uses of guns involved a criminal being killed. For the most part, these savings in human lives, liberty, and property were being made with few people having to brandish, much less use, their guns. Just the knowledge that they are there has been enough to deter thousands of crimes.[27]

● ● ●

Teenager Kipland "Kip" Kinkel was wearing a trench coat when he walked into the cafeteria in Thurston High School in Springfield, Oregon. He pulled a .22-caliber rifle, and nonchalantly began to spray the startled students, wounding twenty-two and killing two.

One of those shot was a seventeen-year-old varsity wrestler named Jake Ryker, who took a bullet to the chest. But Jake was not so easily put down. At six foot four, he was more angry than hurt.

The gunman "would have probably kept on shooting until he was out of ammo or until he started taking aim and making his shots count," Jake later recalled.

Jake looked and saw the gunman put the end of the barrel point blank to a girl's head and pull the trigger three times. Jake's experience from NRA training classes told him that the sound he was hearing was a rifle clicking on empty chambers. He pulled himself up and charged across the room, sending Kinkel reeling.

"He swore and got up and went after the guy," said Ryker's brother Josh, fourteen, who helped knock Kinkel down. "He was pretty irate."

When others joined him in piling on Kinkel, the gunman pulled a 9mm handgun. Jake ripped it out of Kinkel's hand.

Jake's mother later credited his cool handling of the crisis to his NRA training.[28]

Jake's story is just one of countless examples of how firearms training has helped stop a deadly criminal. In homes, stores, streets, and parking lots, Americans use guns to stop a crime *every thirteen seconds*. This remains the important, and largely untold, side of the story.

A Woman's Best Friend

> Shawnra Pence, a twenty-nine-year-old mother from Sequim, Washington, home alone with one of her children, heard an intruder break into the house. She grabbed her 9 mm, took her child to the bedroom, and when the eighteen-year-old criminal broke into the bedroom, she said, "Get out of my house, I have a gun, get out now." He left and the police caught him. She saved her life and her child's life. It made one brief story in the *Peninsula Daily News* in Sequim, Washington.
>
> —*Senator Larry Craig*

"Fortunately," wrote Jeffrey R. Snyder in his groundbreaking article, "there is a weapon for preserving life and liberty that can be wielded effectively by almost anyone—the handgun. Small and light enough to be carried habitually, lethal, but unlike the knife or sword, not demanding great skill or strength, it truly is the 'great equalizer.' Requiring only hand-eye coordination and a modicum of ability to remain cool under pressure, it can be used effectively by the old and the weak against the young and the strong, by the one against the many."[29]

Handguns are estimated to be the instrument of choice in two-thirds of the defensive uses of guns. For a woman threatened by a big hulking man, there is no better alternative.

In fact, more women than ever before are protecting themselves with concealed firearms. By arming themselves, they are doing more than protecting their own lives and dignity. They are protecting their sisters. Lott found that for every woman carrying a concealed hand-gun, the murder rate for all women in a state or community fell by about three to four times more than one additional man carrying a concealed handgun reduces the murder rate for men.[30]

To put it another way, the word gets out.

Criminals learn to become wary, if not downright respectful, of women.

An armed society, as Robert Heinlein wrote, is a polite society. And that's something we should all want.

Chapter Four

(Real) Homeland Defense
Some Modest Proposals on Terrorism

...the largest mass murder in our history was just committed—
without the use of a single gun! Not a bullet fired!...I can't
stop thinking about this. A thousand gun-control laws would
never have prevented this massacre. What am I doing?
                              —*Left-wing filmmaker Michael Moore*

Those who want to use terrorism as a platform for more gun
control must ignore a very inconvenient fact. Since the September 11, 2001, terrorist attack on America, huge numbers of
Americans have become first-time gun owners.

The *New York Times* reported that in the aftermath of the attacks,
background checks for gun purchases surged, peaking at more than
one million in October 2001. Around the country, firearm instruction classes reported record enrollments.[1] At the same time, donations to the Brady Campaign to Prevent Gun Violence plunged
dramatically, causing that wing of the gun-control lobby to make
major staff reductions (the first such cuts in twenty-seven years).[2]

The antigun crowd will tell you that Americans are reacting out
of fear and base instinct. Is that a fair assessment? One has to admit
that there is little that a firearm can do against many of the potential

new threats our government is warning about, whether "dirty" bombs, or chemical and biological weapons. Shooting back at anthrax won't do a great deal of good.

Still, the reaction of the American people is more considered and based on better information than some editorialists and antigun zealots realize. Since the gun-control lobby has introduced the specter of terrorism into the national debate over guns, we thought it would be instructive to take a little time to ask: *What is the role of the Second Amendment for this level of our national—and personal— defense? Is there a role for guns against terror?*

Public Defense Is *Our* Business

First, let's step back and look at the big picture. The message the terrorists brought home is that we are all combatants now. They can strike us anywhere, at any time and place of their choosing, with all the advantages of a surprise attack. The targets available to them are almost limitless. After all, for the terrorist, their battlefield is as large as the world: an airliner in flight, a skyscraper, a government building, a revered monument, the electric power grid, a dam, an oil refinery, the stock exchange, a museum, a football stadium, a school.

The Second Amendment, however, carries a message of its own: *that in such a war, we should all be empowered to fight back.*

Of course, the instinct of some is to move entirely in the opposite direction. They respond by trying to put the nation into a defensive crouch. However, we cannot turn America into a continental prison compound, with concertina wire and concrete barriers walling off public buildings. Nor can we deploy regiments of security guards around every potential target. If we erect battlements around 10,000 potential targets, the terrorists will simply strike target number 10,001.

The widespread nature of this threat means that today, as more than two centuries ago, defending our country is the business of every American. With this in mind, we offer three guiding principles and a handful of specific proposals.

First: A *Realistic* Foreign Policy

It is important for every American to realize—really, to remember—that we've faced down terrorism before. When the Barbary pirates of the early nineteenth century turned the waters of the Mediterranean into their personal preserve, the kingdoms of Europe—already world-weary and cynical—paid the demanded ransoms and accepted piracy as the cost of doing business.

President Thomas Jefferson did not.

When the Barbary pirates preyed on American maritime commerce, Jefferson dispatched the U.S. Navy and Marines "to the shores of Tripoli" to pay America's ransom in the form of shot and shell, extending an umbrella of protection to U.S. citizens and American commerce throughout the Mediterranean.

A century later, America had to deal with another Barbary pirate, an Osama bin Laden–type character, a thug who styled himself "the Rasuli," who had kidnapped a naturalized American citizen named Ion Perdicaris. America was fortunate enough at that time to have another president of courage and high principle. Rough Rider Teddy Roosevelt had an ultimatum read in Congress: "We want either Perdicaris alive or Rasuli dead."

The message got through. Perdicaris was released—alive.

Terrorism today, of course, is far more lethal, with modern technology that can threaten us at home, and a plentiful supply of fanatics who are not afraid to die. Today's terrorists can strike at America's own shores, in our own cities, buildings, and homes. Today's terrorists spring from international networks and travel the world, use cell phones, laptop computers, the Internet, and electronic banking.

So we must show unwavering firmness in the face of terror. Did America do so prior to September 11? Consider a little summation of the previous administration's record on terrorism presented on national radio by the inimitable Paul Harvey. He read:

> After the 1993 World Trade Center bombing, which killed six and injured one thousand, President Clinton promised that those responsible would be hunted down and punished.

After the 1995 bombing in Saudi Arabia, which killed five U.S. military personnel, Clinton promised that those responsible would be hunted down and punished.

After the 1996 Khobar Towers bombing in Saudi Arabia, which killed nineteen and injured two hundred U.S. military personnel, Clinton promised that those responsible would be hunted down and punished.

After the 1998 bombing of U.S. embassies in Africa, which killed 224 and injured five thousand, Clinton promised that those responsible would be hunted down and punished.

After the 2000 bombing of the USS *Cole*, which killed seventeen and injured three U.S. sailors, Clinton promised that those responsible would be hunted down and punished.

Maybe if Clinton had kept his promise, Harvey suggested, September 11 might have been just another gorgeous late-summer day in America.[3]

So our first line of defense is a government that recognizes that weakness in the face of terror is an invitation to more aggression.

Second: Freedom Is *Never* Negotiable

While we need to give our government every reasonable and effective tool to fight terrorism, we must not give up our basic freedoms. If we do, we fall right into the trap the terrorists have set for us—relinquishing the very freedoms they despise so intensely.

You would think this would be obvious to all. Nevertheless, the gun-control crowd wasted little time, shamelessly exploiting a climate of fear after September 11 to push for more restrictions of our constitutional rights. Media darlings like John McCain, Hillary Clinton, Chuck Schumer, Joe Lieberman, and Ted Kennedy all revised their stalled attack on gun shows and morphed it into an antiterrorist measure—as if Osama bin Laden were dispatching his murderous henchmen to snatch up target pistols and pump shotguns at gun shows in Des Moines and Idaho Falls. Other self-serving politicians pounced on the war on terrorism as the pretext to push the idea of a national identity card, the brainchild of at least one "dot-com" mogul who wants you to carry a card with a microchip that could contain almost unlimited personal information—from your medical and driving records, to income data, shopping and travel history, and yes, gun ownership.

In response to the visceral fear that swept America in the aftermath of our generation's Pearl Harbor, government at all levels and politicians of both parties and all ideological stripes have urged Americans to trade our personal freedoms for greater public security. This is a fool's errand. It is always wrong, in every circumstance, to surrender our hard-won essential freedoms for false promises of greater security.

Don't get us wrong. Everyone agrees we need to support the government's efforts to counter terrorists. Federal law enforcement needs to get smart and cooperate and coordinate with one another. Had the FBI been empowered to crack the laptop of one suspect being held prior to September 11, that attack might never have occurred. And no one denies that the greatest threat to American liberty, of course, remains from terrorism. "The fact is," wrote former attorney general Ed Meese, "liberty depends on security, and freedom as we know it in America depends on eliminating the threat of terrorism from our lives."[4]

However, it is also important to remember that many times in the past, the government has requested special powers to crack a tough case or two—only to keep and use those same powers against more benign targets.

Remember RICO—the antiracketeering statute brought against the Mafia? It was a legal tool of extraordinary power and wide scope based on a nebulous standard of "racketeering" that fell on just this side of constitutionality. It was passed by Congress with the explicit intent of giving prosecutors a unique tool with which to take on the mob. And it worked. Thanks to RICO, the government hacked La Cosa Nostra and many other forms of organized crime to pieces. However, once the government got the upper hand, did it retire RICO? No, it expanded it.

RICO is now a powerful legal weapon used against companies, individuals, and advocacy groups. It has become a common feature of law on managed care, tobacco, and prescription drugs. There are "little RICOs" embedded in state laws. There is even a civil form of RICO, which allows anyone who can afford a lawyer to access the extraordinarily wide powers of a RICO statute to bring defendants and organizations to their knees.

In the war on terror, we must be supportive of our government. However, we must also remember that power, once taken by government, is rarely relinquished. So it is crucial that we remain within a constitutional framework, with judicial review and warrants. And we should take great care that the powers used to prosecute a terrorist today are not used against anyone else tomorrow, be they a "pro-life" demonstrator on the Right, or an advocacy group, from the Sierra Club to the NRA, that simply has the temerity to run a political ad at an "illegal" time.

Third: Guns *Can* Stop Terrorists

While private gun ownership may not be our first line of defense against terror, it definitely has a role to play. To understand why, you need only look at what is going on in Israel today.

Just like Americans, Israelis have responded to terrorism by buying guns in record numbers. In fact, the Israeli Interior Ministry reports once the recent intifada's suicide bombings began, its office was inundated by a 75 percent increase in requests for weapons permits.[5]

Time and again, these firearms in the hands of ordinary Israeli civilians have saved lives. One such incident, reported in the *Miami Herald*, told of Israeli shoppers who noticed a man on a warm day wearing a long black coat.

The stranger, of course, was not the Orthodox Jew he meant to be taken for, but Mohammed Tawfiq Shamall. A bang and a flash of light permeated the shop. At that instant, several shoppers pulled their pistols. One of them pumped five shots into the terrorist. When police arrived, they found a bomb strapped to Shamall's body. It had malfunctioned, but given a few more seconds, Shamall probably could have made the bomb go off, taking out the entire market and everyone with him.

This was not an isolated incident. The Israeli press is thick with similar stories of tragedy averted by one quick-thinking man or woman armed with a gun.

For Israelis, carrying guns to deter terrorists is a way of life. "We all walk around with guns," said one woman settler. "When I go to the park with the children, I take my gun with me."[6]

Let us hope that Americans never need to live like Israeli settlers. But armed Americans have an obvious role in stopping terrorists in their tracks.

If the gun-ban activists of the world have their way, we will have made ourselves far easier targets for criminals and terrorists—and that's just plain idiotic.

And what if, God forbid, someone should succeed in detonating a small, crude atomic device? The social chaos would be unprecedented. All the world saw how Korean merchants, armed (ironically) with the same type of firearms their elected representatives in Congress deride as "assault weapons," protected their stores and brought peace to their blocks during the 1992 L.A. riots. Less noticed, but equally effective, was the role that armed citizens played in stabilizing a community against the crime and looting that followed in the wake of Hurricane Andrew that same year.

In the event of the unthinkable, the National Guard would have its hands full just cordoning off the area and rushing injured people to hospitals. Local police departments would be devastated. While we don't like to think of such a "day-after" scenario, there is no doubt that armed citizens would be critical in stabilizing a wounded society.

Specific Measures

Improve Air Security

In January 2002, security guards at Sky Harbor International Airport in Phoenix, Arizona, intercepted a "suspicious" man attempting to board a flight to Washington, D.C. The man was carrying several dangerous items—a small metal nail file, an object that appeared to be a small arms cartridge, and a curious lump of metal shaped like a star.

After lengthy interrogation and repeated searches, the man eventually was allowed to board his flight, minus the nail file and the cartridge, and proceed to his destination. The security screeners reluctantly let him take the star-shaped piece of metal onto the aircraft with him.

Thanks to the vigilance of these alert airport security screeners, eighty-six-year-old Brigadier General (Ret.) Joe Foss was intercepted and deprived of such threatening objects as a small nail file and an obviously inert dummy cartridge that was drilled through and carried on a key ring as a good-luck charm. The unusually shaped piece of metal was the Congressional Medal of Honor, our nation's highest military decoration.

President Franklin Roosevelt presented the Medal of Honor to Joe Foss in 1943 for shooting down twenty-six Japanese aircraft in the Pacific. Joe Foss was, and remains, a household name for millions of the "greatest generation," the generation that fought World War II, defeated Nazism and Japanese imperialism, and preserved freedom for America and the world. After the war, General Foss went on to become governor of South Dakota—the airport in Sioux Falls is named in his honor—and commissioner of the old American Football League. On the day this American hero was subjected to humiliating indignities at the airport in Phoenix, he was headed to Washington and then to the U.S. Military Academy at West Point. He took his Medal of Honor along to show the Cadet Corps at West Point, hoping to inspire the next generation of American military officers.[7]

Or take the case of Lieutenant Greg Miller, a U.S. Army lieutenant who was denied permission to pass through security with wire clippers at San Francisco International Airport. Lieutenant Miller had a jaw wired shut from a bullet wound he received in Afghanistan. He needed the wire clippers with him at all times in case he became sick and needed to open his jaw to avoid choking.

What kind of an airport security system cannot distinguish between an eighty-six-year-old American war hero, or a wounded war hero fresh back from our war on terror, and another Mohammed Atta boarding an airliner with evil intent? Only a system that has sacrificed all reason and judgment in order to be utterly inoffensive to any one group. General Foss's rough handling is hardly unique.

To be fair, good security does have to pay attention to a wide assortment of people. Anyone tricked into carrying a package for another person could be an unwitting terrorist. Still, it defies reason that so many airport indignities should be heaped on so many gray-haired grandmothers, businessmen, and tow-headed toddlers. Even worse, flight crews report that they are all too often singled out for ham-handed searches by security looking for easy marks to make their quotas. Flight crews call this "gate rape."[8]

"How likely is it that the certified pilot with a military record and a family is going to be carrying a gun with intent to hijack his own plane?" asks Chris Cox. "What would you prefer, to trust your pilot, or wait for the U.S. Air Force to stop your hijackers with a Side-winder missile that would take you out as well?"

Perhaps more than anything else, the repeated inspections of flight crews demonstrate how flawed our airport security system really is.

After all, as the likely suicidal copilot of an Air Egypt flight demonstrated in the late 1990s, if your pilot is against you, no metal detector can save you. We have to put our lives into the hands of pilots, no less than we put our lives into the hands of heart and brain surgeons. America's domestic flight crews—often people with military backgrounds, screened by their airlines and the FAA—deserve our trust, just as one's heart surgeon must be trusted. If they cannot be trusted, then all the airport security in the world is useless.

The bottom line is that airport security, in addition to some random searches, should rely on reasonable traveler profiling in order to reduce risk.

Arm Pilots

Another blind spot is the substandard protection of cockpits in the air. If you think that this gaping hole in our security system has been fixed, then think again. There are 35,000 commercial flights every day in the United States, and fewer than 1,000 marshals available to patrol planes. Nor is this likely to improve. To hire enough marshals to fully protect U.S. flights, as Israel protects its fleet of thirty-five planes, would probably require a $10 billion appropriation.[9]

One logical solution is to arm pilots. But the Department of Transportation has ruled that pilots must not be armed. Columnist Ann Coulter quoted John Magaw, head of the new Transportation Security Administration, as saying that pilots should be prohibited from having guns because "they really need to be in control of that aircraft." Coulter responded, "This is literally the stupidest thing I've heard in my entire life."[10] Despite the opposition of Transportation Secretary Norman Mineta, a grassroots organization of pilots—the Airline Pilots' Security Alliance—has designed a program to screen and train pilots to use handguns aboard aircraft.[11]

Predictably, the antigun lobby is up in arms (rhetorically speaking) over this. Violence Policy Center legislative director Kristen Rand says, "A handgun on every plane would mean that the weapon, by definition, would be potentially available to every passenger: from terrorists to unruly or suicidal passengers. Unrealistic scenarios in which criminals meekly surrender at the mere sight of a handgun shouldn't be our guide. Real life is different."

She went on to say, "Experience also teaches that when police fire their weapons, they sometimes make grave mistakes in deciding when deadly force is justified. It is naïve to believe that pilots will fare any better. Recognizing the simple physics of handgun possession at thirty thousand feet, another serious threat is unintentional discharge."[12]

She is playing on the Goldfinger theory of decompression: a gun discharged in a plane creates a hole that sucks people out into the stratosphere and destabilizes the plane.

But wait a minute. Who better to determine the safety of armed pilots than the 66,000 members of the Air Line Pilots Association? After the Department of Transportation ruled that pilots could not carry arms onto planes, a group of senators introduced a bill to circumvent the bureaucracy and explicitly authorize the arming of pilots. The bill could move quickly, and sail through the House, because it is, well, just common sense.

The legislators behind this bill are taking a stand after examining the evidence. They've learned that other alternatives, like stun guns, are problematic, because they bring down only 30 percent of those hit. As far as depressurizing planes, there are projectiles that are available and designed not to penetrate an airplane's aluminum skin.[13] Experts say that even a number of bullet holes probably wouldn't depressurize an airplane.

What about trusting pilots with this responsibility? It was once common practice. In the 1950s pilots routinely carried guns. William Bonnell, an American Airlines pilot, stopped a hijacker dead in his tracks with a .380-caliber Colt automatic in a holster kept in his flight bag. It was 1954. "I had a maniac on my plane," Bonnell said later. "We had women and children. What the hell could a guy do?"[14] So he used his gun.

In fact, commerical pilots were once required to be armed when the aircraft carried U.S. mail. Many pilots with military records have undergone background checks for high-level security clearances, and are trained in the use of firearms. A well-designed program could select pilots and train them in appropriate firearm use. We should arm pilots—the faster, the better.

A similar program of background checks and training could also allow selected enforcement officers (active, retired, and off-duty) to carry firearms on commercial aircraft—thereby meeting the nation's need for sky marshals at little cost. Currently, state and local law enforcement may carry firearms aboard, but only when traveling for duty. And the fact that no special ammunition is required for aircraft travel by authorized law enforcement gives lie to the phony, scare-scenario arguments detailed above.

Get Control of America's Borders

While the ruling elite hungers to impose national ID cards on American citizens, they often overlook the way in which the application of information technology to our borders could make our country safer, without compromising our constitutional rights.

Tracking illegal aliens in America is another appropriate use of technology. The INS has, by all accounts, done a lousy job in the past. Eight million illegal aliens live in the United States—up from less than half that number a decade ago.[15] Most of them are desperately poor people simply looking for a better way of life. But hidden among them are surely some who—like some of the hijackers of September 11—use our lax immigration security as a screen.

Just as we should strictly enforce gun laws against criminals, so too should we better be able to track those who broke the law to be here—while leaving the naturalized, law-abiding immigrant (and native-born American) free from ID cards and other forms of intrusive tracking.

Enlist the Second Amendment

The Second Amendment, far from being a cause of terrorism, is an antidote to terror. As we have seen time and again, an armed society is one that is prepared to repel aggressors. This was true in Revolutionary America, where a ragtag militia of farmers, cobblers, and blacksmiths kept America free. This is true of Israel today. This can be true in the twenty-first century, when the fate of a shopping mall may rest in the hands of a woman with a gun in her purse; the fate of an airline may rest in the hands of an armed pilot; the fate of an American city may rest in the hands of an alert citizenry.

It is more than misguided to restrict our Second Amendment rights because of terror—it is counterintuitive and counterproductive.

In the face of terror, we need the Second Amendment as never before.

Chapter Five

Gun Safety

Store guns so they are not accessible to unauthorized persons. Many factors must be considered when deciding where and how to store guns. A person's particular situation will be a major part of the consideration. Dozens of gun storage devices, as well as locking devices that attach directly to the gun, are available. However, mechanical locking devices, like the mechanical safeties built into guns, can fail and should *not* be used as a substitute for safe gun handling and the observance of all gun safety rules.

—*NRA Gun Safety Rules*

John and Carole Price lost their thirteen-year-old son to a gun accident. The boy had been playing at the house of his father's friend when a nine-year-old playmate picked up a handgun from a dresser drawer and accidentally shot his friend to death.

As happens with many parents who lose a child, grief drove the Prices to activism. In this case, they invested their energies in a very productive form of activism—safety education. If they couldn't save their own child, at least they could save the lives of other children.

The need for such activism is great, for such accidental shooting deaths are entirely preventable. Addressing them should be a simple matter of educating both parents and children. However, as the

Prices learned, nothing in America is simple—not when politics and ideology can come into play.

With the impassioned testimony and lobbying of the Prices, a bill to teach gun safety to state schoolchildren passed the Maryland House of Delegates—a bill that would have made it the first state that required firearms safety instruction for students. To be candid, the bill did not have an easy birth. It was the product of considerable wrangling between the National Rifle Association and gun-control groups. After some false starts and wary discussions, we got down to business, ironed out our differences, and came up with a consensus bill that passed the Senate as well.

For once, it seemed, everyone would come together. For the good of Maryland's children, both sides had bent over backwards. As a result, the legislators crafted a bill requiring children, K through sixth grade, to learn about firearm safety. Students from the seventh to the twelfth grade would be offered safety lessons in firearms. Schools (most likely those in rural areas) could elect to offer students the option of hunting lessons—again, with an emphasis on safety.[1]

It was a rare alignment of planets. However, one major player was out of the alignment—the largest planet of all. Parris Glendening—the Maryland governor who had so embarrassed himself with his awkward fumbling at his gun-lock press conference—vetoed this bill, one that had been supported by Second Amendment activists and proponents of gun control alike.

His reason?

"I have reservations about explicitly sanctioning, and arguably encouraging, the sending of busloads of thirteen-year-old boys and girls to a shooting range to handle real guns and ammunition," Glendening explained in a letter to legislative leaders. "For many young impressionable children, handling weapons in this setting may lead to a heightened interest and contribute to the glorification of guns in our society."

The truth is, the kind of glorification he is talking about already saturates society in many forms of video violence, in which guns neatly dispatch victims with sprays of fake blood. Any young person who has been to a firing range, and operated a firearm under the watchful gaze of an instructor, leaves with a lifelong impression that firearms are not toys. They leave with a sense of respect for firearms and understanding of the skills needed to operate them safely and effectively—the opposite of "glorification."

Glendening went on to say, in a press statement, that he was troubled that the legislation would have allowed the National Rifle Association to work with school boards to develop safety curriculums.[2]

What is it that so disturbed the governor's conscience? Is the NRA turning children into gun-toting fiends? Is it Eddie Eagle? At the heart of the NRA's gun-safety program, Eddie Eagle is a benign mascot, a cartoon figure on videotape and costumed instructor who visits schools. Since 1988, the NRA has spent more than $100 million on gun safety, imparting Eddie Eagle's lifesaving message to more than fifteen million schoolchildren in fifty states. This message, designed by some of the nation's leading child psychologists and experts on elementary curricula, is a masterpiece of simplicity:

If you see a gun: STOP! *Don't Touch.*
Leave the Area. *Tell an Adult.*

Eddie Eagle teaches this mantra in a singsong style that children easily learn by heart. Reduced to its basics, this program instills the developmentally appropriate notion in a child's mind that young children should no more touch a gun than put a finger on a hot stove. It has been so effective that it has won the endorsement of the National Sheriffs' Association. Patricia Kunz Howard, RN, looked at the more than eighty gun-safety programs and evaluated them on nine criteria, ranging from "critical safety" elements to consideration of "cultural diversity." Her published study gave the highest marks to Eddie Eagle. The usefulness of the program has been recognized by state legislatures, the National Safety Council, and the Police Athletic League.

The program is having measurable effects. The National Center for Health Statistics reports that firearm-related fatalities for children have declined 88 percent from 1975 to 1999. The Chicago

Transit Authority and Chicago Housing Authority wrote us to report that some local children saw guns under a mattress and immediately ran to tell adults, instead of playing with them—probably saving lives. Eddie Eagle is a runaway success that should be duplicated in every school in every state.

Why would anyone have a problem with Eddie Eagle? He is not political. He is not ideological. He doesn't use safety instruction to teach the NRA view on the Second Amendment to children. There is never a firearm present during his lessons. All Eddie Eagle does is save lives. Who could be against that?

Many gun-control organizations—whose worldviews are opposite ours—understand and agree that as long as people are allowed to have guns, safety is an important consideration. Only an extremist, opposed to the very existence of guns, would be willing to sacrifice the safety of children in order to be ideologically pure.

Another extremist is former New York City public advocate Mark Green, recently defeated in his bid to become mayor. When a city police officer showed an Eddie Eagle video to schoolchildren, Green went berserk: "I think the NRA has blood on its hands. I think they are morally and legally responsible for thousands of deaths a year, in a sense, in our city and our country, and they should not be anywhere near our kids talking about guns."

This is the same mentality as that of the Violence Policy Center, which opposes safety training because it might encourage people to own firearms and because "the majority of such training would inevitably be conducted by NRA-certified instructors."[3] The VPC event went so far as to equate Eddie Eagle with Joe Camel, claiming that Eddie Eagle encouraged kids to shoot much as Joe Camel encouraged them to smoke. Of course, the VPC did not mention that while the cartoon Joe Camel has a cigarette in his mouth, Eddie Eagle *never* picks up a firearm.

In other words, it doesn't matter if this program works or not—we just don't like the NRA.

For the rest of us, people of all political stripes, safety—not ideology—is paramount. For those of us who care about safety, not scoring points, here's what you need to know.

You must make your guns absolutely inaccessible to unauthorized users—whether they're your children or others. This may mean gun locks (though, as we discussed in Chapter Two, these locks have their drawbacks). This may mean a gun safe. If you need advice on making this decision, come to the "safety" portion of our NRA.org Web site, or contact your local firearms retailer to review available products. It would be best if you could enroll in a gun-safety program. The point is, if you need guns for your personal safety or want them for recreation, you *must* know how to properly operate and store them for your own safety and for that of your family.

After all, gun ownership is a responsibility as well as a right.

Of course, the Glendenings and Greens of the world want to change this balanced equation: They want you to have all responsibility and no rights. They cannot seem to grasp that firearms have an overall beneficial effect on society. One reason some people don't realize this is that the success of guns in warding off criminal violence is rarely portrayed in the media—since the incident doesn't result in a camera-ready crime scene. Only a fraction of 1 percent of the protective use of firearms results in the fatal shooting of a criminal. By definition, the success of guns in deterring 2.5 million crimes a year produces no body count. We can tell you, however, that the use of firearms to deter criminals is three to five times the estimated number of violent firearms crimes committed every year.[4] The only body count here is the number of living, healthy Americans walking around whose lives, property, and dignity have been saved.

What about child accidents? In 1995, many more children were killed in motor vehicle crashes (2,900), drownings (950), and fires (1,000) than from firearms accidents (30 deaths of children up to age four, 170 up to age fourteen). In fact, more children are killed by bicycle accidents than are killed by firearm accidents. We don't ban bikes, notes John Lott, because people need the exercise for health and enjoyment. We don't ban heaters, because they keep people from getting sick and freezing to death.

The same is true for guns. They protect homes and save lives.

What about "smart guns"? Do they constitute a "have your cake and eat it too" solution? These are guns with biometric or other high-tech identifiers that allow only a designated user to fire them. However, this technology is not anywhere near the stage at which it could be commercially reliable. A 1996 report to the National Institute for Justice could give only a "B" to the highest-ranked prototype. No police force we know of is ready to trust the lives of its officers to smart guns—even though law enforcement is the intended market for such products (given that police shootings often involve the officer's own sidearm).

"There's no such thing as a smart gun," Chris Cox says. "If law enforcement isn't interested, why should homeowners be told they need it?"

One world-renowned firearm manufacturer, Beretta, whose gun-making heritage harks back to 1526, recently issued a statement: "In our opinion, such technology is undeveloped and unproven. In addition, Beretta strongly believes that 'smart gun' technology...could actually increase the number of fatal accidents involving handguns."[5]

As we said in previous chapters, one accidental shooting is one too many. The answer, of course, is to continue to drive down the phenomenal decrease in these numbers of accidents to the ultimate goal of zero. This is where education comes in as a critical element. Even gun controllers should agree (and many do) that as long as there are guns in our society, there should be gun education. Surely, we should all be able to agree on that much.

Eddie Eagle—or someone very much like him—should be allowed to impart an indelible impression on every child.

The Twilight of Sportsmanship

What about the rest of the Maryland bill—was Glendening right to disallow children the right to gun-safety instruction and safe hunting courses? Let us turn to two great Americans, both of them "Teds," to respond.

The first is the guitar wild man known to millions as "The Nuge." Ted Nugent, in addition to being one of the great musical talents of the last few decades, is also a dedicated family man and hunter who offers the following prescription. He says: "Had America continued with quality control of disciplined gun safety education as did our forefathers up through the 1960s, coupled with commonsense law enforcement and a justice system that recognizes something resembling justice, I believe we would not have to be scrambling for such apparent damage control now. Part of this desperate need for last ditch damage control is a result of denying the gun's historical and unavoidable allure." He goes on to call for "Ballistics 101" for students, taught by specially trained "law enforcement officers, retired military personnel, even qualified volunteers, who can communicate in a proven effective manner and style to each age group."

In the absence of such programs, adults need remedial education—a gap the NRA is striving to meet. Nationwide, the NRA has 38,000 instructors and coaches who conduct programs in firearm safety and proficiency. Every year, we reach more than 700,000 people of all ages.

Such education was once an integral part of our heritage. A second great American, the other "Ted"—President Theodore Roosevelt, NRA life member and winner of the Nobel Peace Prize—spoke to this need when he concluded his Sixth Annual Message to Congress, on December 6, 1906. He wrote: "We should establish shooting galleries in all the large public and military schools, should maintain national target ranges in different parts of the country, and should in every way encourage the formation of rifle clubs throughout all parts of the land. The little Republic of Switzerland offers us an excellent example in all matters connected with building up an efficient citizen soldiery."

These two Teds—Roosevelt and Nugent—understood that at the heart of this instruction is something much more than firearm safety. It is a sense of self-reliance, character, and skill that used to be called sportsmanship. And it is precisely this ethos that is the real target of gun-control extremists.

Consider, for example, what these extremists have to say about hunting—a sporting activity as old as the Republic, as American as the Fourth of July, one that has been passed on from parent to child from the beginning of time.

Ingrid Newkirk, cofounder and president of People for the Ethical Treatment of Animals (PETA), one of the most active animal extremist groups, with direct links to the terrorist Animal Liberation Front:

- "I don't believe human beings have the right to life. That's a supremacist perversion. A rat is a pig is a dog is a boy." —*Audubon*, November 1990
- "Even if animal tests produced a cure [for AIDS], we'd be against it." —*Vogue*, September 1989
- "Six million people died in concentration camps, but six billion broiler chickens will die this year in slaughterhouses." —*Washington Post*, November 13, 1983
- "You can't legally deface someone's property—but if you're somewhere and no one's looking, go ahead." —*Animal Rights 1997 Conference*, July 1997
- "Pet ownership is an absolutely abysmal situation brought about by human manipulation." —*Harper's*, August 1988

Wayne Pacelle, vice president of the Humane Society of the United States (HSUS), which operates out of Washington, D.C., and "strongly" opposes any type of hunting:

- "If we could shut down all sport hunting in a moment, we would." —*Associated Press*, December 30, 1991
- "We want to stigmatize hunting, we see it as the next logical target and we believe it is vulnerable." —*Field & Stream*, June 1991
- "Having hunters oversee wildlife is like having Dracula guard the bloodbank." —*Field & Stream*, June 1991

Michael W. Fox, senior scholar, the Humane Society of the United States:

- "We're not superior. There are no clear distinctions between us and animals." —*Washingtonian*, February 1990
- "The life of an ant and the life of my child should be granted equal consideration." —*Inhumane Society*, 1990

Cleveland Amory, the late founder of the Fund for Animals, a New York City–based group that focuses on getting animal extremists appointed to state wildlife commissions:

- "Hunting is an antiquated expression of macho self-aggrandizement, with no place in a civilized society." —*U.S. News & World Report*, February 5, 1990
- "These bloodthirsty nuts claim they provide a service to the environment. Nonsense! A hunter goes into the woods to kill something, period." —*U.S. News & World Report*, February 5, 1990

Dave Foreman, cofounder of Earth First!, a radical environmental group based in New York and New Mexico:

- "I think the whole concept of private property as an ultimate good has got to be replaced. There's a higher good out there than private property." —*Animal Rights Reporter*, June 1989

Rod Coronado, Earth First! and Animal Liberation Front, a group whose terrorist acts in the United States can be traced back to 1982:

- "Launch your own campaign against the fur industry.... Find a fur shop in your area and smash or etch its windows. Liquid steel ruins locks; bomb threats only cost a quarter. If you live in an area where furs are worn, fill a squirt bottle with red dye or battery acid and let fly. If you're presentable enough to get into a fur shop department store, take a razor blade and slash the coats." —*Earth First! Newsletter*, Vol. xii, #2, 1991

These are not just people who fail to understand the role of hunting in much of American life. These are people who, by their own admission, cannot distinguish between the life of an ant and the lives of their own children. Their opposition to gun ownership is part and parcel of a larger campaign to transform America into the image of one or another idiosyncratic utopia. Look beyond the slick advertising, and more often than not you will find "gun-safety advocates" and other gun controllers in bed with these antihunting zealots.

For a heartland perspective, we can do no better than, once again, turn to Teddy Roosevelt.

Encouragement of a proper hunting spirit, a proper love of sport, instead of being incompatible with a love of nature and wild things, offers the best guaranty for the preservation of wild things.

—*President Theodore Roosevelt*

No one had more moral authority to speak out on conservation than TR, the president who saved so much of our nation's natural heritage and treasured parks. He understood that hunting is an important wildlife-management tool. It certainly is a mainstay of our environment today. According to Representative Don Young of Alaska, dollars collected from hunters have been used to purchase millions of acres of public land. Through ten thousand clubs and organizations, from the NRA to Ducks Unlimited, sportsmen contribute $300 million each year to wildlife-conservation activities. In fact, hunters and fishermen fund nearly 75 percent of the annual income for all fifty state conservation agencies—more than $20 billion in all.

The NRA has been successful in promoting wildlife conservation on federal, state, and local levels. We have protected hunting from legislative and regulatory assault in all fifty states. We steadfastly oppose every effort by those who detest sportsmanship to outlaw or pass onerous restrictions on hunting.

- For information about Eddie Eagle, a program that teaches children to stay away from guns, call (800) 231-0752 or log onto www.nrahq.org/safety/eddie.
- For an NRA safety video for adults, *Personal Protection in the Home*, call (800) 336-7402 and request item number ES 26838.
- To find a home firearm safety course near you—how to handle and store guns safely—call (800) 672-3888.

We hold that hunting expresses an American need to stay connected to the land. It allows parents to pass on a heritage, providing not only recreation, but also sustenance. More important, it is about a way of living, of taking responsibility, of placing ourselves in nature and society.

And we hold that hunting, done properly, is completely safe.

If those who profess such a concern for safety were as enthusiastic in supporting tough measures against criminals with guns, instead of going after hunters and gun-safety programs, this would be a very safe country indeed.

Chapter Six

Second Amendment Follies

When the resolution of enslaving America was formed in Great Britain, the British Parliament was advised by an artful man, who was governor of Pennsylvania, to disarm the people; that it was the best and most effectual way to enslave them; but that they should not do it openly, but weaken them, and let them sink gradually.... I ask, who are the militia? They consist now of the whole people, except a few public officers.

—*George Mason, 1788, Virginia Ratification*
Debates on the U.S. Constitution

On a bright spring morning in May 2002, Solicitor General Theodore Olson—the Bush administration's lawyer to the U.S. Supreme Court—filed a motion informing the high court that the administration was going to reverse the Clinton-Gore Justice Department interpretations that the Second Amendment protected only a "collective right."

"The current position of the United States ... is that the Second Amendment more broadly protects the rights of individuals, including persons who are not members of any militia or engaged in active military service or training, to possess and bear their own firearms," Olson wrote. That right, he added, is "subject to reasonable restrictions designed to prevent possession by unfit persons or to restrict the possession of types of firearms that are particularly suited to criminal misuse."

Olson was reinforcing the view of Attorney General John Ashcroft, who wrote the National Rifle Association in 2001: "While some have argued that the Second Amendment guarantees only a 'collective' right of the states to maintain militias, I believe the amendment's plain meaning and original intent prove otherwise."[1]

What does it all mean? What did the Justice Department under Clinton mean by a collective right? For that matter, what *is* the meaning of the word "militia" in the Second Amendment?

The debate over history, original intent, and fine shades of meaning is not a debate over academic questions. As the Bush administration clearly understands, these questions are at the heart of what kind of society we want to be.

The Second Amendment reads:

"A well regulated Militia, being necessary to the security of a free State, the right of the people to keep and bear Arms, shall not be infringed."

Twenty-seven words.

Four phrases.

And whole libraries full of commentary telling us what it all means.

Do you have to be a member of a militia in order to enjoy a right to a firearm? Is a militia what we would now call the National Guard? Must it be well regulated in order for the right to come into play?

At a time when an artful dodger can dissect the meaning of the word "is," there is ample room here for word games. Some have tried to argue that the Second Amendment is not an individual right at all. One prominent historian won the most prestigious literary prize in his field by asserting that gun ownership itself was alien to early Americans.

These games, however, come to a stop when one consults the people whose opinions count most—the Founders. Their voluminous writings and heroic life stories give us an unambiguous guide to the meaning of the Second Amendment.

"A Divine Animal Right"

James Madison, Thomas Jefferson, and others who played an integral role in developing the Bill of Rights and the U.S. Constitution, lived in an age when all public intellectuals were fully versed in the classics, steeped in the literature of ancient Greece and Rome.

Most of them held to a classical concept known as natural law. In its most basic expression, natural law means that to be human is to possess inherent rights, such as the right to free speech, the right to worship as you choose, the right to assemble with others. These human rights may be a gift of God or nature. Whatever their origin, they are yours from birth. They are an indelible part of you. And any government that fails to respect them is, by definition, illegitimate.

One of these sacred natural rights, respected by philosophers in ancient times, is your right to self-defense.

Cicero—the great Roman senator who sacrificed his life in a struggle against tyranny—defined this principle for all time, a law that comes "not by instruction, but by natural intuition. . . . I refer to the law which lays it down that, if our lives are endangered by plots or violence or armed robbers or enemies, any and every method of protecting ourselves is morally right."[2] Other classical thinkers—from Plato and Aristotle to Ovid, Livy, Horace, and Marcus Aurelius—wrote about the fundamental human right of self-defense.

To put this idea in contemporary language, flash forward—way forward, from the classical to the modern, from high culture to pop culture. In a recent Jennifer Lopez movie, *Enough*, Lopez's character is being chased with her daughter all over creation by a homicidal ex-spouse. She is told, "The cops can't help you. No one can help you. He's gonna keep coming until he kills you." At one point in the film, a strong woman delivers to Lopez's character one of those stunning lines that echo in your mind long after the movie itself is forgotten. She is told: *"You have a divine animal right to protect your own life and the life of your offspring."*

If you scour classical literature, from Aristotle to Augustine, you couldn't do a better job of boiling down the essential meaning of your natural right to self-defense. The Founders themselves—born as British subjects—held this view, and they held it with passion. They also had a deep appreciation, born as subjects of the British Crown, of the way in which English common law recognized this right.

The right to keep and bear arms was first put in statute in the reign of Henry II in A.D. 1181. The Assize of Arms of that year, along with subsequent statutory decrees, such as the Statute of Winchester of 1285, made the right of armed self-defense a matter of common law and royal pronouncement.

By the time of King Charles II, popular ownership of weapons was so entrenched among commoners that when the king attempted to restrict these rights in the 1670s with the Game Act, under the pretext of preserving royal game, he met with widespread resistance. The real motive was to disarm the British people so he could impose his personal rule upon them. These restrictions were joyfully abandoned during the subsequent Glorious Revolution of 1688, which sought to abolish the standing army and reinstate the right to keep and bear arms. The Declaration of Rights, signed February 13, 1689, by William and Mary upon their ascension to the British throne, set forth the basic rights enjoyed by all their subjects, including the right of the people "to have Arms for their Defence."

Like the Magna Carta of 1215 and the U.S. Constitution, this declaration became a model for our Second Amendment. When proposed, the original language of the act included the phrase "common Defence." The declaration was finally adopted, and signed by William and Mary, with the deletion of the word "common." Clearly, the British had evolved an individual right, not a "collective" right linked to national defense.

By the eighteenth century, the great English jurist Sir William Blackstone would observe that Englishmen securely possessed "the right of having and using arms for self-preservation and defence."

So what did our American Founders mean when they put quill to parchment to define this right for Americans? Once again, what did they mean by a "well regulated Militia" and "the right of the people to keep and bear arms"? The real meaning of their words is brought home when one surveys the literature of the people who were behind the American Revolution.

In proposing a constitution for Virginia in 1776, Thomas Jefferson declared, "No free man shall ever be debarred the use of arms." Not a militia, or a group of men. He said "no free man." How much plainer can it be that Jefferson was thinking of individual rights?

What about a "well regulated Militia"? Again, a careful reading of the Founders leaves no doubt that by "militia" they are referring to the population of American adults. We are the militia because we are responsible for securing our own freedom. We are responsible for regulating ourselves.

"Who are the militia?" asked Tench Coxe of Pennsylvania, friend of Benjamin Franklin and early abolitionist. "Are they not ourselves? Congress have no power to disarm the militia. The swords and every other terrible implement of the soldier, are the birthright of an American." He also wrote that the militia are "in fact the effective part of the people at large."[3]

These words and thoughts are echoed, time and again, by virtually all the Founders. Even Alexander Hamilton, proponent of a standing army, said that such an army would not be a threat to liberty as long as there is "a large body of citizens, little if at all inferior to them in discipline and the use of arms, who stand ready to defend their rights and those of their fellow citizens."[4]

Some have tried to explain away the Second Amendment as a "collective right." The Founders could not have been more explicit in making it clear that it is an individual right.

We are the militia.

Our right to keep and bear arms cannot be taken away from us.

And the Founders clearly meant for our possession of arms to be an insurance policy to make sure that the government respects our liberty.

Today, the individual right to keep and bear arms is guaranteed not just by the U.S. Constitution, but by the constitutions of forty-four states as well, each of which has a provision specifically protecting that freedom.

The Modern Debate

Another way to understand your Second Amendment rights is to view them in the context of the rest of the Bill of Rights. Larry Craig, senator from Idaho, takes a hard look at the collectivist interpretation and finds it wanting.

In a speech on the Senate floor, he said: "[U]nder this [the collectivist] standard, the Bill of Rights would protect only the right of a government to speak, or the right of a government to criticize itself, if you were taking that same argument and transposing it over the First Amendment. In fact, the Bill of Rights protects the rights of people from being infringed upon by government—not the other way around."

That's why they call it the Bill of Rights. It is meant to protect our rights as citizens from the government, not the government's rights from citizens.

Senator Craig continued:

> [The framers] made the Second Amendment the law of the land because it has something very particular to say about the rights of every man and every woman, and about the relationship of every man and every woman to his or her government.
>
> That is: The first right of every human being, the right of self-defense.
>
> Let me repeat that: The first right of every human being is the right of self-defense. Without that right, all other rights are meaningless. The right of self-defense is not something the government bestows upon its citizens. It is an inalienable right, older than the Constitution itself. It existed prior to government and prior to the social contract of our Constitution. It is the right that government did not create and therefore it is a right that under our Constitution the government simply cannot take away. The framers of our Constitution understood this clearly. Therefore, they did not merely acknowledge that the right exists. They denied Congress the power to infringe upon that right.

Moreover, Senator Craig said, this social contract that is the Constitution of the United States explicitly tells the Congress that it will *never* have the authority to take this right away. "Further," he noted, "the framers said not only does the Congress not have the power to abolish that right, but Congress may not even infringe upon that right. That is what our Constitution says. That is what the Second Amendment clearly lays out. Our Founding Fathers wrote the Second Amendment to tell us that a free state cannot exist if the people are denied the right or the means to defend themselves."[5]

This interpretation by Senator Craig, Attorney General Ashcroft, and Solicitor General Olson is not an extremist one. It is a moderate, sensible adherence to the obvious intent of the Founders. It is an interpretation that has been endorsed repeatedly in legislation approved by the U.S. Congress and signed into law by presidents such as Franklin Roosevelt and Ronald Reagan. The real extremists are those who would mute or mutilate this enumerated constitutional right.

These are the same people who, for sixty years, have been trying to erode the Second Amendment into meaninglessness through court interpretations. But this same crowd received quite a jolt in October 2001—not from the Bush administration, but from the judiciary.

This came in a blockbuster court decision, with tremendous aftershocks being felt throughout the judiciary and American politics. The U.S. Court of Appeals for the Fifth Circuit ruled in *U.S.* v. *Emerson* that the Second Amendment protects an individual right to keep and bear arms. Most of the 40,000-word decision, written by Fifth Circuit senior judge William L. Garwood, is a ringing endorsement of the conventional, individual-rights interpretation.

The court concluded:

> We have found no historical evidence that the Second Amendment was intended to convey militia power to the states ... or applies only to members of a select militia. ... All of the evidence indicates that the Second Amendment, like other parts of the Bill of Rights, applies to and protects individual

Americans. We find that the history of the Second Amendment reinforces the plain meaning of its text, namely that it protects individual Americans in their right to keep and bear arms whether or not they are a member of a select militia or performing active military service or training.

With these words, Judge Garwood tumbled the pillars of the legal school that holds to a collective-rights interpretation—that gun rights belong only to state militias (which today, some argue, is the National Guard). He also noted another popular theory, one spun by some liberal judicial activists, called the "sophisticated collective-rights" theory. This theory admits that the Founders intended individuals to have *some* rights, but they had to be exercised within the context of some form of collective defense.

The judge concluded: "We reject the collective rights and sophisticated collective rights models for interpreting the Second Amendment. We hold, consistent with [*U.S. v.*] *Miller*, that it protects the right of individuals, including those not then actually a member of any militia or engaged in active military service or training, to privately possess and bear their own firearms."

The only exceptions, the court noted, were "limited, narrowly tailored specific exceptions or restrictions for particular cases." In other words, it is constitutional to deprive convicted felons, among others, of their Second Amendment right. This is in keeping with *U.S. v. Miller*, a Supreme Court case often mistakenly cited by the Reno Justice Department and other liberals as supporting a "collective-right" view.

Far from being a gun controller's dream, *Miller* upheld the National Firearms Act of 1934, which restricted heavily certain types of weapons (like sawed-off shotguns). On close examination, these restrictions turn out to be "narrowly tailored specific exceptions" of the sort Judge Garwood would later discuss. In *Miller*, the Supreme Court defined the militia in explicitly individual terms. The high court ruled in 1939 that "the signification attributed to the term Militia appears from the debates in the [Constitutional] Convention, the history and legislation of Colonies and States, and the writings of approved commentators. These show plainly enough that *the Militia comprised all males physically capable of acting in concert for the common defense.* . . . Ordinarily when called for service these men were expected to appear *bearing arms supplied by themselves* and of the kind in common use at the time [emphasis added]."

Imagine, *Miller* is the best ruling that gun controllers have had to hang their theoretical hats on for the last sixty years. After *Emerson*, they have nowhere to go. Now defendants around the United States, accused of violating local gun-control laws, are arguing that their constitutional rights take precedence. In some cases, the defendants may win on principle but lose on the facts—some of them are convicted violent criminals who, under any interpretation of the law, would and should be deemed "unfit" to carry firearms. What is important from a national standpoint is that the underlying constitutional principle be upheld by the courts.

One such test case could easily arise in Washington, D.C., with its sweeping restrictions. "The D.C. law is absolutely vulnerable," said scholar Robert Levy of the CATO Institute. "It's so broad, so across-the-board, that no one can own a handgun, period. It doesn't allow for reasonable regulation."[6]

When Solicitor General Olson filed his brief, he was merely formalizing the end of the debate.

Daniel Boone's Popgun

You have to hand it to them. The antigun folks are nothing if not tireless and inventive. Having clearly lost the struggle to reinterpret the plain meaning of the U.S. Constitution, they are now adopting another tactic.

They are trying to sell the notion that the reliance of early Americans on firearms is a myth. According to this theory, very few Americans owned firearms of any sort in the decades before and after the Revolution. There were few gunsmiths, guns were rare, and most that were around did not work. The traditional view that guns played a significant role in the founding and westward expansion was wrong. The Minutemen, the hardy frontiersmen that James Fenimore Cooper wrote about, the farmer with a rifle displayed over the hearth—all that was no more real than Washington's cherry tree.

How could some commentators become so deluded about the past? These revisionists say that it wasn't until gun manufacturers like Samuel Colt came along, in the aftermath of the Civil War, that guns became commonplace. National myth-making, they claim, fueled by the advertising of gun manufacturers, sold us on a national gun tradition that really never existed.

In short, having failed to deconstruct the American Constitution, these revisionists went on to try to deconstruct history itself. The champion of this theory is one Michael A. Bellesiles of Emory University.

In September 2000, after a decade of research, Bellesiles published *Arming America: The Origins of a National Gun Culture*. Bellesiles became an overnight, if unlikely, celebrity. The liberal establishment on the university campuses and in the prestige media greeted this politically correct thesis with wild acclaim. *Arming America* showed that the terms of the gun debate were founded on misguided notions and that America's "gun culture" rested on mythic fallacies.

Two eminent historians lavished praise on the book. Garry Wills praised it on the cover of the *New York Times Book Review*, as did Edmund Morgan in the *New York Review of Books*. Then *Arming America* won the Bancroft Prize—the most prestigious literary prize for historians. For an academic historian, this is as good as the Nobel.

"This award is well-earned," said Michael Barnes, president of Handgun Control, Inc., and the Center to Prevent Handgun Violence. "Professor Bellesiles has produced a work of unquestionable historical and societal merit. The National Rifle Association and its allies rely on a mythology about guns and the Second Amendment because they have few legitimate, rational arguments. By exposing the truth about gun ownership in early America, Michael Bellesiles has removed one more weapon in the gun lobby's arsenal of fallacies against common-sense gun laws."[7]

But while gun-control extremists and academic historians went wild, doubts about the book began to grow among amateur historians and defenders of the Second Amendment. When complaints began to arise about Bellesiles's sources and methods, few professional historians took notice. They were confident they had caught the "gun lobby" manipulating American history to serve a political agenda.

Soon, however, doubts and details began to put Bellesiles and his compatriots on the defensive. Even the universal media acclaim and praise from liberal academicians began to wither in the face of scrutiny. Independent historian Clayton Cramer systematically dismantled much of Bellesiles's research in *American Rifleman*, revealing blatant misrepresentations and distortions. In many cases, Bellesiles had asserted that his sources said the exact opposite of what the record shows. In other cases, he ignored evidence from his own main sources that ran counter to his thesis. In yet other cases, Bellesiles ignored important primary sources that refuted his argument.

While the academic community was slow to react, other Second Amendment defenders continued to pick apart the flawed research. Michael Korda, the legendary editor-in-chief of Simon & Schuster and a noted writer in his own right, published a critical review in *American Rifleman*.

Korda wrote: "What we are seeing with *Arming America* is another familiar example of history being rewritten to make the past conform to the media's prevailing opinion of the present. In the meantime, those who read this book should do so with a cautious and skeptical eye, since, like all sweeping generalizations about the past, it reflects the prejudices of the present."[8]

Other skeptics combed through *Arming America* and found shocking lapses of professional judgment. Melissa Seckora wrote a series of devastating investigative articles on *Arming America* in National Review Online. (It made no news, however, because it ran on September 11, 2001.) She followed up with another piece in November, saying, "Some of the most significant statements in *Arming America* are 'based' on data that do not exist." She focused her laser-like attention on the portions of the book that dealt with the West:

Documents Bellesiles told me he reviewed at the San Francisco Superior Court were actually destroyed by fire in the
1906 San Francisco earthquake. When I told Professor Bellesiles that the probate records could not be found at the San
Francisco Superior Court, he changed his story: "Did I say San
Francisco Superior Court? I can't remember exactly. I'm working off a dim memory. Now, if I remember correctly, the Mormon Church's Family Research Library has these records. You
can try the Sutro Library, too."

But the records do not exist at the Sutro Library; nor does
the Mormon Church's Family Research Library have an archive
that Bellesiles purports to have used. The library's supervisor
of public affairs has said that the library has an index of all
estates in probate in the city and county of San Francisco from
1850, but the index does *not* list information about gun ownership. In fact, anyone who knows anything about probate
records from San Francisco County agrees that the records do
not exist.[9]

In the pages of *American Rifleman*, Clayton Cramer noted Bellesiles's theory that in early America "hunting was very rare here until
the mid-1830s when a small number of wealthy Americans chose to
ape their upper-class British counterparts." If this was true, Cramer
noted, "it seems a bit odd that the Provincial Congress was ordering
every militia member to be armed and the towns to provide arms to
those who didn't have them." He added, "The Provincial Congress
of Massachusetts bought arms from many private owners in the first
few months of the war, sometimes purchasing as many as one hundred in a single transaction." And, Cramer stated:

Somehow, Bellesiles read Rush Baynard Hall's memoir of
frontier Indiana life immediately after statehood (1816)—and
missed Hall's detailed description of how hunting was a common part of life for most settlers, done partly for sport, and
partly because it supplied fresh meat at very little expense. Not

surrounded by guns? Hall devotes an entire chapter to the joy of target shooting with rifles.

The rifle was so common an implement and target shooting so common a sport, that when Hall went out evangelizing in a sparsely settled part of Indiana, one of his fellow preachers switched in mid-sermon to a metaphor involving rifle matches to sway the audience.[10]

Another writer in *American Rifleman*, Stephen P. Halbrook, reported that Thomas Jefferson owned and used dozens of firearms in his eighty-three years. From 1773 to 1800, he purchased at least three long guns and eight pistols. Halbrook wrote: "Bellesiles also ridicules the marksmanship of the militiamen at Lexington and Concord because the 3,763 Americans shot only 273 Redcoats (yet British regulars hit just 95 Americans). Lt. Frederick Mackenzie of the Royal Welsh Fusiliers, who was there, disagreed: 'These fellows were generally good marksmen, and many of them used long arms made for Duck-shooting.' By contrast, the Department of the Army estimates that U.S. forces in Vietnam expended 50,000 rounds to cause a single enemy casualty."[11]

The *New York Times* finally had to take note of the growing controversy in December with a long story detailing the burgeoning scandal surrounding the tarnished academic superstar. The intellectual Maginot Line became impossible to defend.

One of the severest critics of *Arming America* was James Lindgren, law professor at Northwestern University. Professor Lindgren was particularly deadly to this book because he is himself a proponent of gun control, and is not part of the "jihad of ideological nitpickers" Bellesiles says is behind the critiques of his book. Lindgren found "dozens of serious errors" in *Arming America*, for which Bellesiles offered implausible and contradictory explanations.

Finally, the criticism reached a level where it could no longer be ignored in the faculty workshops at Columbia, Yale, and other universities. The controversy convinced Emory to order Bellesiles to provide a "detailed, point-by-point" response. Melissa Seckora reports that Don Hickey, a Wayne State College history professor who peer-reviewed Bellesiles's earlier work, said: "These criticisms have convinced me that Bellesiles misread, misused, and perhaps even fabricated some of his evidence. I no longer believe that his evidence proves his thesis (though it is still possible that the thesis is at least partly correct). Had it not been for the work of an independent scholar as well as the popular press, I might not have reached this conclusion."

One Emory University professor told Seckora that "Bellesiles's response is utterly responsive." Though the academic world is rife with talk of disciplinary action, Columbia has not at this writing revoked the Bancroft Prize, and the publisher, Knopf, insists that the criticisms are a "matter of interpretation." Chicago's Newberry Library awarded Bellesiles a $30,000 fellowship funded by the National Endowment for the Humanities (NEH). In May 2002, the NEH demanded that its name be removed from the fellowship. Slowly but surely, this academic scandal is moving forward to disclosure.[12]

The point of this little tale is not to add to one man's disgrace. It is to note the glee with which an uncritical media and liberal academic establishment celebrated this work of pseudo-scholarship. It is this same elitist disregard for the Second Amendment that makes so many hungry for "cop-killer bullets," "assault weapons," and other "facts" that simply are not true.

The Second Amendment in Action

Perhaps you saw a PBS "reality" miniseries that chronicled the lives of three families as they attempted to live like 1883 homesteaders. The father of one such family, Gordon Clune, became alarmed at how much weight he and his children were losing. From washing, to farming, to preserving food, the Clunes lived just as our pioneer ancestors did, with only one exception. They were allowed to do no hunting.

Clune, who had enrolled in gun-safety classes before taking on this assignment, was told he had strict limits on how to use guns to ward off hostile varmints. "We were supposed to give a predator two warnings," he told the *Los Angeles Times*. "'Excuse me, Mr. Coyote, please don't eat my chicken. Excuse me, Mr. Coyote, please don't eat my chicken.' Then you were supposed to fire a warning shot."[13]

When the American Minutemen answered Paul Revere's call to arms, they picked up their muskets and Pennsylvania long rifles and hurried off to Lexington and Concord. What was the spark that had finally ignited this revolution against King George III? Nothing less than a British attack on the right to keep and bear arms.

When the Redcoats assembled on Boston Common and marched off toward Lexington and Concord, they were after Americans' arms. The British intended to seize the arsenals of Massachusetts and confiscate gunpowder and shot. Although our public schools may no longer emphasize this inconvenient fact of American history, the Revolution was ignited by a direct assault on the ancient English right of the people to keep and bear arms.

The story of self-defense in America begins with that fact. It is buttressed by Paul Revere's ride, the Sons of Liberty, the fighting on Lexington Green and at Concord Bridge. Each Minuteman owned his own musket or rifle, a bayonet, a cartridge box, and thirty rounds of ammunition. Many veterans of the Indian wars on the frontier threw hatchets.

While America would embrace the right of the common man and woman to arms, the mother country—source of our original concepts of liberty—began to slip. Britain's Bill of Rights and Constitution may exist in statute and common law. They are, for the most part, unwritten. And that makes them susceptible to tinkering by statute, without resort to our elaborate process of amendments and ratification.

In 1900, a British prime minister opined that there should be a "rifle in every cottage." By the time of Dunkirk some forty years later, when the island nation faced the prospect of invasion, the British people had been effectively disarmed by the gradual encroachment of gun control. In a subtle and gradual way, the terms of their ancient constitution had been altered.

When the war came, and it appeared Britain might be invaded, they had no recourse but to appeal to Americans to send pistols, rifles, revolvers, shotguns, and binoculars to the besieged British. The U.S. government was asked to send huge Lend-Lease shiploads of military rifles. Among the arms that went to Britain was a rifle sent by a "Yank" who happened to be a world-class sharpshooter, John Hession. The rifle he sent was a prized match rifle, an M1903 rifle, .30-06-caliber modified for long-range competition. Hession had used it in many international sporting events, including Olympic competition. Now he had sent it to the British army with a plaque attached to it with the following inscription: "For obvious reasons the return of this rifle after Germany is defeated would be deeply appreciated."[14]

Winston Churchill would later recall in his memoirs: "When the ships from America approached our shores with their priceless arms, special trains were waiting in all ports to receive their cargoes. The Home Guard in every county, in every village, sat up through the night to receive them.... By the end of July we were an armed nation."[15]

Britain, of course, did not remain an armed nation. In the decades after the war, gun control returned with a vengeance. The country that had given birth to this form of liberty relinquished it, probably for all time.

The American Bill of Rights, because it is written down in bold ink, has proven harder to toss aside.

Chapter Seven

The Gun-Control Hive

Ideally, handguns should be banned completely, but we recognize that this strategy is not currently politically feasible.

—Dr. Jeremiah Barondess

"When an isolated, terrible event occurs, our phones ring, demanding that the NRA explain the inexplicable," says our good friend and colleague, NRA president Charlton Heston. "Why us? Because their story needs a villain. They want us to play the heavy in their drama of packaged grief, to provide riveting programming to run between commercials for cars and cat food.

"The dirty secret of this day and age is that political gain and media ratings all too often bloom upon fresh graves.

"I remember a better day, when no one dared politicize or profiteer on trauma. We kept a respectful distance then, as NRA has tried to do now. Simply being silent is so often the right thing to do."

In the search for villains, the gun-control community often goes to wild extremes. Former FBI agent and author Gary Aldrich reported that an Ohio University professor of journalism, Patrick S. Washburn, came under intense attack for displaying a Civil War relic on his office wall. The rifle, used by his great-grandfather, is utterly inoperable. Nevertheless, someone accused him of violating the university's "workplace violence" policy. Soon he had armed campus policemen at his door. At this writing, he faces possible disciplinary action.

The professor fought back with humor. Ohio University's football team has a small cannon that it fires to signal a touchdown; the professor announced that presumably this was a weapon that should also be forbidden by campus policy. Aldrich noted that in a day when rapes and worse occur on every campus, the attention on a decorative antique is somewhat beside the point. "What causes some otherwise rational people," he asked, "to go off the deep end with nonsensical policies that are obviously selectively enforced?"[1]

The answer, of course, is that no one is really going off the deep end. Both Dr. Washburn and Charlton Heston can tell you that the antigun crowd is pursuing a very conscious strategy. They want to socially isolate and stigmatize—and demonize—the opposition.

Scholar John Lott can tell you what it is like to be demonized. With the naïveté of a scholar concerned with scientific truth, he circulated galleys of his original, groundbreaking article for the *Journal of Legal Studies* to gun-control groups. To his surprise, he had trouble interesting Susan Glick of the Violence Policy Center in commenting on his related talk to the Cato Institute, a think tank in Washington, D.C. She didn't even want him to send her his paper for an advance review. Lott writes:

> However, when the publicity broke on the story with an article in *USA Today* on August 2 [1996], she was among the many people who left telephone messages immediately asking for a copy of the paper. In her case, the media were calling, and she "need[ed] [my] paper to be able to criticize it." Because of all the commotion that day, I was unable to get back to her right away.
>
> ABC National Television News was doing a story on my study for that day, and when at around 3:00 P.M. the ABC reporter doing the story, Barry Serafin, called saying that certain objections had been raised about my paper, he mentioned that one of those who had criticized it was Ms. Glick. After talking to Mr. Serafin, I gave Glick a call to ask her if she still

wanted a copy of my paper. She said that she wanted it sent to her right away and wondered if I could fax it to her. I then noted that her request seemed strange because I had just gotten off the telephone with Mr. Serafin at ABC News, who had told me that she had been very critical of the study, saying that it was "flawed." I asked how she could have said that there were flaws in the paper without even having looked at it yet. At that point Ms. Glick hung up the telephone.

Lott soon found himself under attack for not submitting the article for peer review, although he had sought many reviews for months before the paper was accepted for publication.[2]

Such coordinated attacks do not appear out of thin air. They come when opponents can muster large, disciplined organizations and are media-savvy and rich in human resources. These are the same forces that have an uncanny ability to provide the filter through which countless media leaders—editors, producers, and reporters—see the world. These organizations are many, but they often act as one. They are backed by some of the world's wealthiest people, the world's most powerful corporations, and the world's most famous celebrities. In the last election cycle, they established two little-noticed, below-the-radar "get-out-the-vote" organizations funded with $1 million each.[3]

Who are these people?

The Brady Campaign and the Brady Center to Prevent Gun Violence: This is the old warhorse of gun-control activism, the gun-ban group, formerly known as Handgun Control, Inc., founded in 1974. Jim and Sarah Brady became affiliated with HCI in 1985 and became so integral to the operation that it assumed their name in 2001. This organization has had a number of successes in generating hysterical news coverage and persuading the Congress and states to crack down on nonexistent problems ("cop-killer" bullets in 1986) or undertake perverse actions (the original Brady Bill that once required an onerous five-day waiting period in 1993, and scaring Missouri voters into rejecting a concealed-carry provision in 1999). Based in Washington, D.C., this group in the last presidential election had half a million members and spent up to $4 million to influence politics through contributions, independent expenditures, and issue ads. Chaired by Sarah Brady, with the leadership of CEO Michael D. Barnes, a former Democratic congressman from Maryland, the organization supports the efforts of a subsidiary, the Center to Prevent Handgun Violence, in its efforts to sue gun manufacturers out of business.[4] Despite its wealth and sophistication, the Brady Campaign has shown signs of disarray after its ham-handed attacks during the 2000 elections on George W. Bush backfired.

The Million Mom March: Everyone remembers the stern visage of Rosie O'Donnell leading the activist Million Mom March (MMM) on Washington. It was meant to appear as if it were a spontaneous, grassroots uprising by angry soccer moms. In fact, the MMM is a very sophisticated organization, started by an anonymous donation of $1 million. It is intensely political, working very closely with the Brady groups to make the difference in closely contested House elections, and to influence federal and state legislation. Before September 11, it had 80,000 names on its mailing list and 250 chapters across the country.[5]

The Violence Policy Center: Most gun-control groups are aware of the need to disguise much of their agenda. The Violence Policy Center (VPC) is the most absolutist of the antigun groups in openly calling for a ban on handguns, and it is also the most forthright about its real agenda. The VPC vision is so restrained by ideological blinders that it routinely opposes and demonizes education programs, like Eddie Eagle, because it sees gun-safety education as placing "the onus of safety and responsibility on the children themselves."[6] For all its lack of guile, VPC can command some attention. Late in the Clinton administration, it put together a coalition to give the Treasury Department authority to regulate guns as consumer products. This coalition included the American Bar Association, the Consumer

Federation of America, the NAACP, and Physicians for Social Responsibility.[7]

Doctors Against Handgun Injury: This coalition purports to be concerned only about guns as a health issue. They were a major force in prompting doctors around the country to ask people about guns in the house. However, the group's Web site lists among its positions many that sound more political than medical: expand the Brady background checks to gun shows, severely limit the number of guns an individual can purchase, restore the waiting period, make your gun ownership part of your medical history (part of a record they would share with a national Centers for Disease Control database).[8] Dr. Tim Wheeler, a California surgeon who heads a rival group, Doctors for Responsible Gun Ownership, responds, "It's clear that these physicians are working from a political agenda against gun owners, and therefore, that question becomes inappropriate. Any doctor who asks a patient an intrusive and politically motivated question about guns in the home is committing an ethical boundary violation, and that doctor should be disciplined." When interviewed by Morley Safer of *60 Minutes*, Wheeler produced an article written by Dr. Jeremiah Barondess, a leader of the "guns and health" coalition who argued that handguns should be banned completely, although "we recognize that this strategy is not currently politically feasible."[9]

This is part of a wider movement within the American Medical Association (AMA) to use its clout on Capitol Hill to push gun-control activism. The centerpiece of the AMA's effort is to persuade the Centers for Disease Control to extend the Clinton-Gore philosophy to treat gun ownership, essentially, as a disease. As this 155-year-old organization moves further left, it loses clout and members. Thirty years ago, the AMA represented 75 percent of all physicians; today it represents only 29 percent. "They have not done a good job in Washington," says Dr. Arnold S. Relman, former editor of the *New England Journal of Medicine*. "They've been manipulated by politicians, and they've been caught in internal scandals."

You would think that as its budget implodes, its members flee, and its influence diminishes, the AMA would get off this hobbyhorse and on to something critical to its existence, like tort reform.

Americans for Gun Safety: Andrew McKelvey, the billionaire sponsor of Americans for Gun Safety (AGS), is a seasoned hand at gun control. "He pumped millions into Handgun, Inc., and got nowhere," Chris Cox says. "He's a bottom-line guy—trying to get a return on his investment." Represented by the benign images of Senators John McCain and Joseph Lieberman, AGS is the sleek newcomer. AGS is the leader of the campaign to confuse voters into seeing gun ownership in America as a threat from international terrorism. Funded by its sole billionaire backer, it has zero members and no gun-safety programs. Nonetheless, it is spearheading the charge to make gun shows impossible in America. Though brand new, AGS is fast becoming a trendsetter. A survey of other groups' Web sites shows them moving quickly to ape parts of the AGS agenda. Because of its sophisticated advertising and moderate "hunter-friendly" image, AGS is potentially the most lethal of all the gun-control groups.

How can organizations like these be so active? None of them can begin to compare to the millions of dues-paying men and women who are members of the NRA. The antigun axis of power is financed and supported by an "iron triangle" of three forces:

- VRIs (Very Rich Individuals)
- Nongovernmental organizations (NGOs) and foundations
- Corporations

The VRIs: Among the Very Rich Individuals who make the modern gun-control movement possible is one that the reader was introduced to in the first chapter—Andrew McKelvey, the retired dot-com billionaire. His brainchild, AGS, is headquartered in the "Gucci Gulch" corridor of the Washington, D.C., lobbying district. Its staff roster reads like a Who's Who of former Bill Clinton and

Andrew Cuomo staffers. McKelvey's professed interest in a non-ideological approach is belied by these hires. However, as the successful businessman that he is, McKelvey seems to know what it takes to win—hence his bankrolling of the soothing, warm-as-butter organizational image.

Another VRI is George Soros, the Hungarian émigré who became a billionaire through currency-exchange deals. He has invested his money in a plethora of oddball initiatives, including needle-exchange programs for addicts, and euthanasia. "There are areas where there's a bigoted approach, as for instance in drugs," Soros told a reporter. "There are areas we just refuse to deal with, like the problem of dying. In those areas, I am fostering debate." He funded a successful measure, California's Proposition 215, which decriminalized the use of marijuana for medical purposes. He also funds programs to change the position of the Catholic Church on abortion.

Soros has made mega-contributions to help plaintiffs' attorneys target gun manufacturers. He has emerged as a major sugar daddy of the gun-control community.[10]

There are, of course, many smaller VRIs, centimillionaires whose massive individual contributions allow these organizations to act as if they had broad-based, popular support.

NGOs and foundations: Foundation money has long been an irony of American life. Usually set up by philanthropic capitalists, these groups evolve over the years into left-wing support groups that would make many of their founders roll in their graves (although more recent foundations have been born out of the hard-left convictions of their founders). The Violence Policy Center, which advocates stricter gun-control measures than Sarah Brady's Handgun Control, Inc., receives more than 90 percent of its money from such foundations as the George Gund Foundation, the Joyce Foundation, and the ultraliberal MacArthur Foundation.[11]

When Handgun Control, Inc., listed "campaign partners" in 1995, it revealed support from some of the nation's largest and best-known nongovernmental organizations. Some are obviously liberal organizations comfortable with the Brady message. Some, like the AFL-CIO, are obviously going against the strong majority opinion of their rank-and-file. Others included the American Association of School Administrators, the American Bar Association, the American Civil Liberties Union, Common Cause, the American Federation of Teachers, Americans for Democratic Action, the Gray Panthers, Public Citizen, United States Conference of Mayors, and the YWCA of the U.S.A.

Corporations: Did you know that familiar corporations that make some of your favorite products are also bankrolling the gun-control movement? They range from Michael Eisner at Disney to Sara Lee, Sprint, and Time Warner, as well as openly liberal companies like Ben & Jerry's ice cream and Levi Strauss. Think about that the next time you slip into a pair of jeans, scoop some ice cream, warm up a few brownies for the kids, and sit down to watch *Pocahontas*.

The professional gun-control movement is not a grassroots movement coming to life. It is an effort funded by VRIs, foundations, and corporations, supported by the left-leaning leaders of national organizations, and given the spotlight by antigun celebrities. Together, they constitute a hive of continuous antigun propaganda and agitation, a continuous buzz of political appeals and political influence.

But what motivates them to such persistent action? They all share one thing in common—a desire to exert social control in order to create Utopia.

Utopia, of course, does not exist. It never has. It's an imaginary place, invented in 1516 by Sir Thomas More, the famous "Man for All Seasons." More's book described a fantasyland, an ideal community where everything was peace and harmony, where all lived according to the law, where crime, poverty, want, need, greed, envy, and all other vices were unknown. The longing to create a perfect society is an old one in human history. It has inspired all kinds of social experiments, from monasticism in Europe to America's communal groups like the Amish. We have also seen the dark side of utopianism in the last century. The Soviet Union was an experiment in creating a Marxist utopia, the Workers' Paradise. Hitler's Germany was an expression of fascist utopianism, the perfect Aryan state purged of imperfections. Mao's China, the killing fields of Pol Pot's Cambodia, Castro's hopelessly backward Cuba—most totalitarian schemes have been experiments in utopianism. And all have deprived their people of the right to self-defense.

Our own homegrown utopians in America may not put their ideology in such stark terms as those in other countries, but the instinct is unmistakably in the direction of social control. The utopians cannot bear freedom. They cannot trust that most individuals, if left alone, will make the right choices. Utopians are the elite who know best how people should live and order their lives. They are wiser, smarter, more caring than the rest of us—or so they believe. They see themselves as superior both morally and ethically. If the utopians cannot persuade people to voluntarily embrace their notions about how society should be structured, they are prepared to use coercion to achieve their objectives.

This is why they are willing to take away our guns. And this is why they are eager to use technology—including ID cards—to keep track of our individual choices. In business school, it is often said that what you can measure, you can manage. In politics, what you can track, you can control.

On the other hand, freedom is messy. It's about millions of people making their own decisions about their own lives, how and where they will live, what work they'll engage in, what they will teach their children. The utopians hate freedom—especially the Second Amendment. This is not because there is anything to fear from law-abiding gun owners, but because an armed people are able to resist the potentially violent coercion of the utopians and their social engineering schemes to remake society according to their delusions of perfection. Disarm the people and they would be powerless to resist.

Whether it's the animal-rights fanatics of PETA, the anti-cheeseburger cops of the Center for Science in the Public Interest, or any of the other utopian dreamers who want to rule our lives, they are all animated by the same impulse.

They are all frustrated by freedom.

So, in the final analysis, the gun-control movement is about power. Who will have it? Who will exercise it?

In the chapters ahead, we will examine the various arenas in which this collection of groups is working to restrict our freedom.

We will look at how they have used the power of plaintiffs' attorneys in an attempt to achieve through lawsuits and civil law what could not be achieved through legislation.

We will look at their power in Hollywood, and how they use their celebrity spokespersons and media dominance to brainwash America.

We will see how this hive is increasingly acting on the international stage, using multilateral organizations like the United Nations as platforms for their views.

Finally, we will take a look at the political landscape and assess the threat of these groups in the years ahead.

Chapter Eight

The Litigation Machine

If lawyers file and finance lawsuits against an unpopular industry and then channel billions of dollars of booty back into government treasuries, while also channeling millions more into soft-money donations to political parties, how is that any less corrupting than when chemical companies make PAC contributions in exchange for tax breaks? ...

If the Left ceases to be a counterweight to huge concentrations of unaccountable private wealth and power, of what earthly use is it? And what will remain of its credibility if its best friends are billionaire lawyers? Answers: none, and not much.

—*Jonathan Rauch*, National Journal

The trial lawyer has emerged as the pop-culture hero of our times. Think of how many movies and television shows glorify the exploits of the trial lawyer—from *Erin Brockovich*, to the *Rainmaker*, to ABC's *The Practice*.

For all their differences, these shows present simple morality plays. Corporations and other big institutions are always greedy monsters that value profits over human life. Trial lawyers—who are always scripted to have some charming peccadilloes to be forgiven by the viewer—are the ones who can restore justice to poor people damaged by (fill in the blank).

These are also David and Goliath stories, the rumpled trial lawyer who can barely afford to keep himself in coffee and yellow legal tablets standing up to slick, powerful legal moguls of the defense bar, the dreaded corporate lawyers who have the personality of Klingons. Somehow, against the odds, the little guy always manages to win the day.

The reality is starkly different, for it is the trial bar that has become Goliath. Some trial lawyers have a net worth that can be counted in the billions. You can understand why when you consider that about one hundred law firms will split the $10 billion legal fees of the recent tobacco settlement. Trial lawyer Peter Angelos owns the Baltimore Orioles. Texas lawyer Joe Jamail is one of the richest men in America.[1]

"These people fly around in bigger jets than we do," one insurance executive told *Business Week*. "This is no longer a cottage industry."[2]

While trial lawyers work the courtrooms, their millions of dollars in contributions to the political system help elect members of Congress, state legislators, judges, and mayors who work the halls of power. What do they want? They want compliant lawmakers who will pass laws that make it easier to extract even more money out of the productive economy.

One form of litigation alone—asbestos—is projected to eventually cost the U.S. economy some $200 billion. That's four times the liability of the September 11 terrorist attacks.[3] In all, the annual cost of the American tort system is equal to 2 percent of our total national wealth.[4] In fact, trial lawyers are so wealthy that they are not only buying up big-ticket items like baseball teams and wineries, but are also emerging as a major financial presence in Hollywood—bankrolling the very pictures that convince the national jury pool that they're the good guys. It's all very neat.

So what, you're wondering, does all of this have to do with guns?

Trial lawyers have become so powerful that they've begun to replace many of the functions normally undertaken by the legislative and the regulatory process. Legal scholar Walter Olson calls trial lawyers "an unelected fourth branch of government."[5] How can they do this? Consider this—when a jury in New Mexico awards a humongous settlement to a woman who spilled coffee on herself, a lawyer is using twelve people, in effect, to act as a national legislature to mandate tepid coffee for everyone else. As trial lawyer wealth grows, so too does the scope of their ambitions. They are no longer interested in the temperature of coffee. They are combining forces with public officials, like state attorney generals and mayors, to use the court system to create binding national policies.

Here, as with McCain's "campaign finance reform," you see an instinct toward control—getting away from the messy business of democracy, with its long-winded debates, its weather-vane policy twists, and its troublesome constitutional restrictions. Let's get down to the business of changing the world in earnest, they seem to say, without bothering with the vagaries of public opinion or Robert's Rules of Order. So, as you might have guessed by now, one of the things trial lawyers have set out to do is to make it practically impossible to make or buy a gun in America.

Hypocrisy on Stilts

Trial lawyers have joined forces with liberal, big-city mayors to launch mega-bucks lawsuits against gun manufacturers. From Philadelphia to New Orleans, big-city mayors have joined in alliances with trial lawyers to hold gun manufacturers responsible for the misuse of their products.

This effort has not gone smoothly. A New York jury, in one of the first of these suits, failed to hold a Tennessee-based gun company responsible for a shooting. "We're not happy with the fact that these gun companies exist," one juror told the *New York Post*, "[but] they didn't pull the trigger."

By basing its decision on common sense, that New York jury showed restraint. However, it takes only one jury out of many to come back with a big, precedent-shattering verdict to set the stage for the virtual takeover of an entire industry. With the threat of a bet-your-company lawsuit in his pocket, then mayor Ed Rendell of

Philadelphia began pressuring gun manufacturers in the late 1990s to sign on to a laundry list of gun-control policies.[6] Soon, George Soros, the MacArthur Foundation, and other deep-pocket gun-control promoters were funding dozens of suits on behalf of cities.[7]

Sure enough, by February 1999, they got their breakthrough case. A Brooklyn jury found three gun makers liable for the criminal misuse of their products. Not only did this jury breach the concept of individual responsibility, it held these three gun makers *collectively responsible* because the police could not determine which one of them made the gun in question.

So in one legal decision, the trial bar established the collective guilt of an entire industry—for acts it did not commit.

Another favorite legal theory—one that gained ground across the country in the late 1990s—was that gun makers are liable under "public nuisance" statutes: an utterly novel interpretation of the law that puts local ordinances above the Second Amendment of the U.S. Constitution.

In one sixty-six-day period in 1999, New Orleans, Chicago, Atlanta, Miami, and Bridgeport, Connecticut, added to the blizzard of lawsuits against gun manufacturers. Attorneys worked hand-in-glove with these mayors, and also with the Center to Prevent Handgun Violence, the 501(c)(3) arm of the Brady group. These five suits have sought to enforce this new form of collective guilt, in which all gun makers would be held "collectively liable" for damages by any of their peers. Part of this strained, new argument was that guns are inherently unsafe because gun makers do not use "personalized" technology that would prohibit nonowners from firing them (never mind that such technology is years away from being reliable, not to mention affordable).[8]

Another landmark case came in early 2002, when an Illinois appellate court ruled that gun makers and dealers can be sued for distributing firearms in a way that makes it easy for criminals and juveniles to obtain them, a practice that creates what the court says could amount to a public nuisance. The decision ignored the reality that gun makers comply precisely with the thousands of restrictions put on them by Congress and state legislatures. It is hard to see how gun makers and dealers could be better policed. But that is beside the point. "Gun control groups," reported Fox Butterfield of the *New York Times*, his personal glee seeping into the copy, "hope the Illinois decision could lead to successful lawsuits against an industry that has been largely immune to them."[9]

To buy into the logic of these suits filed by mayors, one must overlook polls of the rank-and-file police under them who work the streets. They consistently favor gun ownership for the law-abiding. One must overlook the results of a survey of 15,000 police chiefs and sheriffs conducted by the National Association of Chiefs of Police—93 percent thought law-abiding citizens should be able to purchase guns for self-defense.[10]

Most astonishing of all, antigun mayors overlook the fact that they themselves rank among the major distributors of the nation's guns. In jurisdictions ranging from Boston, to Detroit, to Alameda County, California, authorities routinely conduct "gun swaps" to defray the cost of new police equipment. Boston—which endorses the novel legal theory that private vendors are showing "willful blindness" to what happens once guns are sold—itself attached no strings to resales when it rid itself of some 3,000 handguns several years ago. New Orleans worked through an Indiana broker to recycle some 7,300 guns—including the TEC-9s banned by Congress in 1994.

"For hypocrisy, it's hard to top that," notes Walter Olson.

For the trial bar, it is not enough, of course, to rely on a pliable jury. Trial lawyers, cycling a fraction of their one-third take in damage awards back into political contributions, are seeking—and receiving—the kinds of laws they need to make their suits easier.

One example is the Unsafe Handgun Act signed into law by California governor Gray Davis in 1999. This serves the purpose of focusing a jury's attention on the gun, as a matter of product law, instead of the intent of the person who uses the gun. In short, California is one jury decision away from holding products and their

manufacturers—not individual perpetrators—accountable for crimes.
California is moving steadily toward new law and punitive measures
against target groups.[11]

Return to Reason

While the NRA represents gun owners—not gun makers—it doesn't
take a genius to see that all this litigation is gun control by another
name. Recognizing this, the NRA swung into action in states ranging from Georgia, to South Dakota, to Louisiana, to prevent cities
from using tort law to create gun control.[12] George W. Bush, in his
second term as Texas governor, signed such positive, protective, pro-
gun legislation into law.[13] In all, twenty-seven states have passed laws
prohibiting cities and counties from suing gun makers under public-
nuisance laws.[14]

Businesses of all sorts are seeing that public-nuisance antigun laws
can be misapplied to a multitude of products and are forming defensive coalitions. Think tanks, like the National Center for Policy
Analysis in Dallas, are getting into the act—performing the research
to show that cities benefit much more from the defensive use of guns
than they suffer in gun violence.[15]

Judges in appellate courts are also beginning to weigh in on behalf
of the Second Amendment.

Mayor Marc Morial of New Orleans, rebelling against the restrictions of the Louisiana legislature on public-nuisance laws, went to
court to try to have the pro-gun law overturned. The Louisiana
Supreme Court had another view. In 2001, it declared that the city's
"lawsuit constitutes an indirect attempt to regulate the lawful design,
manufacture, marketing and sale of firearms." It then went on to
remind New Orleans that only individuals have constitutional rights,
not cities. It dismissed the suit—a decision upheld by the U.S.
Supreme Court.[16]

In 2002, a federal appeals court in Philadelphia struck down another
lawsuit from the gun-control crowd, with the court explicitly denying
that gun makers could be sued for creating a "public nuisance."

At this writing, other appeals look promising.

The constitutions of forty-four states recognize the right to bear arms. In recent years, the NRA has been successful in persuading forty-two states to enact preemption laws that prevent local jurisdictions from imposing ordinances that are more restrictive than our state constitutional rights.[17] Preemption of silly, baseless litigation intended to harass a legitimate industry was a natural next step. On the federal level, bills are pending in both chambers of Congress to preempt such lawsuits nationally.

The tide has turned. But it can turn again. We have to remain alert, at the treetops level of national tort law, and at the grassroots level of city hall. There will always be some inventive legal theorist looking for a novel way to gut the plain meaning of the Second Amendment in a courtroom.

Chapter Nine

Hollywood and Guns
Scarface and Sanctimony

"I don't care if you want to hunt, I don't care if you think it's your right. I say 'Sorry.' " And to cap off this stunning display of jurisprudential obtuseness, Ms. O'Donnell added that, in what was then apparently her ideal world, "you are not allowed to own a gun, and if you do own a gun I think you should go to prison."

—*M. Christine Klein, writer and attorney,*
on comments by Rosie O'Donnell

Ever watch *West Wing*?
It is a slick, well-done show, fast-paced and engrossing. It is also a peek into the inner mind and most heartfelt desires of the Hollywood liberals who write and produce it. It is, in truth, a wistful look back at what the Clinton administration could have been if Bill Clinton had not been personally corrupt, and not been eager to adopt parts of the agenda of a Republican Congress in order to cling to office.

One aspect of the show, however, is pure Clinton nostalgia—every few episodes, President Josiah Bartlet (Martin Sheen) gets an opportunity to mount his high horse against guns in America. In one recent episode, he reacted with sputtering moral outrage after a madman shot up a church in Texas. Just to make the storyline as ironic and as difficult as possible for Second Amendment advocates, the writers threw in a little girl who died when hit by a stray bullet—not one fired by the crazed gunman, but one fired by a bystander in the pews who happened to be carrying a gun under the Texas concealed-carry law.

Of course, this being entertainment and not a policy seminar, President Bartlet did not bother to ask the fundamental question— one that is also applicable to the policy question of arming commercial pilots. If a madman—beyond the reach of any law—did come into your place of worship and begin shooting, would you actually just want to sit there and wait to die? Or would you be grateful that someone could shoot back? And if you were on one of the doomed planes hijacked by terrorists on September 11, would you have wanted the pilots to have had access to a firearm? One thing you can be sure of, *West Wing* will never depict a real Texas tragedy—Luby's cafeteria—as it actually happened. Nor will you get a virtual tour of the soundstage the show is filmed on—complete with the ring of armed security guards who protect highly paid stars from the streets of Los Angeles.

If we were in other countries, we would all right now, all of us together, all of us together would go down to Washington and we would stone [House Judiciary Committee chairman] Henry Hyde to death. We would stone him to death! Wait! Shut up! No, shut up! I'm not finished! We would stone Henry Hyde to death and we would go to their homes, and we'd kill their wives and children. We would kill their families.

—*Actor Alec Baldwin,* Late Night with Conan O'Brien

Hollywood remains a wholly owned subsidiary of the far Left, sometimes the loony Left. There is certainly no denying the deep connection between Hollywood and the extremes of the gun-control movement. The fingerprints of big media can be found, for example, all over the Million Mom March. The organizer, Donna Dees-Thomases, is often portrayed as a New Jersey housewife outraged over school shootings. In fact, Dees-Thomases was a high-powered publicist at CBS and sister-in-law of Susan Thomases, Hillary Clinton's lawyer, political advisor, and *consigliere* who persuaded her to run for the Senate. Rosie O'Donnell was recruited to emcee the march. Hillary herself appeared on David Letterman's late-night show to promote the event. And the event itself kicked off with the organizers' triumphant march across the White House lawn, complete with full media access. Though the Million Mom March came nowhere near recruiting one million women, it was indeed a publicity success—which you'd expect for an event stage-managed by media liberals. But the policy goal of scaring suburban women into an antigun frenzy failed miserably. Nowhere in the media will you find an accurate portrayal of the Million Mom March group today—broke, defunct, with only the name bought out by the Brady Group to save face.

Hollywood Hypocrites

Larry Elder, libertarian talk-show host and author of *The Ten Things You Can't Say in America*, recently put together a Who's Who of gun-control hypocrisy for Hollywood stars. One of them is actress Sharon Stone, who asked others to turn in their firearms. "I urge you to trust and believe in your local law-enforcement officials," she said, "and to trust and believe in the courage of following your heart and surrendering your fear and anger." Yet, Elder notes, Stone had a different opinion when she was confronted by a trespasser. As the actress recalled for *Movieline* magazine, "As [the gate] swung open, I pumped my shotgun and said, 'I'm gonna blow your ass all over the street.' And I heard him land when he jumped and his footsteps running off."[1]

Now come on. If it's all right for you to protect yourself, why not a shop owner who is in fear for his life? So many starlets who would nod in sympathetic agreement with that movie line about a mother having a divine animal right to protect herself and her offspring somehow get hoodwinked into trying to talk other women and mothers out of doing the same.

Another celebrity Elder pinpoints is Geraldo Rivera, who on CNBC said, "How much longer are we gonna be wrapping in the flag of patriotism to justify 250 million guns out there?" Yet when Fox News sent Rivera, with his brother, to cover the liberation of Afghanistan, the Riveras announced they were armed. "We refuse to be crime victims. We're not the victim types. If they're going to get us, it's going to be in a gunfight. It's not going to be a murder. It's not going to be a crime. It's going to be a gunfight."[2]

Perhaps the choicest quote is from Charlton Heston, who, in the midst of the L.A. riots, received calls from one liberal Hollywood friend after another asking to borrow a gun and get lessons on how to shoot it. "I could teach you," he told them, "but not in an hour."[3]

Then, of course, there is Rosie O'Donnell—who could be described as the Queen of Hypocrisy, at least as far as guns are concerned.

Did you catch her ambush interview a few years back, in which she tried to make Tom Selleck squirm over his support for the NRA? Since then, several facts have come to light about Rosie. At the same time she was lashing into Selleck, and leading Million Mom Marches on Washington, Rosie was also serving as a spokeswoman for Kmart—one of the largest gun retailers in the world.

Perhaps she didn't know. Kmart certainly did, and eventually terminated their relationship.

But she had to have known the reasons why she hired a security guard, armed with a gun, to escort her son to public school. She expressed concern, reported in a Connecticut newspaper, that "publicity about her son's attendance at a local school—coupled with the information that the guard would be unarmed—could make him vulnerable to harm." Uhhmm, let's see, no gun, vulnerable, sounds like a pro-gun position to me.

On one recent Halloween she also had a security guard separate the parents of trick-or-treaters from their kids at the front entrance to her gated mansion.[4]

Michael Korda sums it up nicely: "People living in Beverly Hills, with hundred-thousand-dollar security systems and a Colt Python .357 by the bed, are eager to disarm poor African-Americans and Hispanics."[5]

Kids, Movies, Music, and Guns

> Someone should shoot him with a .44 Bulldog.
> —*Director Spike Lee, on NRA president Charlton Heston*

After the Columbine school massacre, Hollywood went into a frenzy of denunciation. One celebrity after another demonized the NRA and lit into Charlton Heston in a very personal, vicious way. One thing you didn't hear about, however, was the link between Hollywood and the tragedy.

After the killings, the police investigated the belongings of Eric Harris and Dylan Klebold. The police discovered that both teens were deeply affected by the Oliver Stone movie *Natural Born Killers*. In Harris's yearbook, Klebold actually wrote about "the holy April morning of NBK." NBK stands for Mr. Stone's opus. The slaughter occurred in April.

J. C. Watts, Republican congressman from Oklahoma, studied the police evidence and concluded that these "killers had filled their spiritual vacuum by making a religion out of violence. Their high priest seems to have been Oliver Stone." Watts went on to say:

> I am not guessing here. We have the killers' word for it.... Can we link the Columbine slaughter to the entertainment industry? Clearly, we can. If a person is caught painting swastikas on a synagogue, and then a subsequent search of his room discovers Nazi literature, don't we assume a link? Of course we do.
>
> Similarly, if a person attacks a citizen of a different race, and a subsequent search of his home finds racist literature, don't we assume there is a link? We would be incredibly foolish not to....
>
> But who has gotten the lion's share of blame for this horror?

The man most to blame, we have been instructed, is Charlton Heston.[6]

For his part, Heston has gone out of his way to bring home the link between violence and material that the big media companies are putting out. Against the advice of family and colleagues, he attended a Time Warner stockholders' meeting and asked for the floor. Once given the mike, Heston read the lyrics of a rap song by Ice-T, "Cop Killer," which celebrates the ambush and murder of police officers. At least one murder of a police officer had occurred since the release of the CD. Heston read:

> I got my 12-gauge sawed off
> I got my headlights turned off
> I'm about to bust some shots off
> I'm about to dust some cops off...

It got worse—much worse, including a graphic depiction of a fantasized sodomizing of two twelve-year-old nieces of Al and Tipper Gore.[7]

Somehow, the entertainment industry lives comfortably in the middle of one giant disconnect. Stars attack our Second Amendment rights, but keep those rights for themselves. Hollywood moguls contribute money to gun-control organizations and lobby for changes in the law, while some of them finance and market movies and CDs that glorify and inspire violence.

We appreciate that danger is an age-old element of drama. *Cape Fear*, *Fatal Attraction*, or the *Panic Room* would lack suspense without a demented killer lurking in the shadows. *Gladiator* would be a mere costume drama without its bloody excesses. *The Patriot* is one of the bloodiest movies in memory—and one of the best. It showed what the clichéd phrase "our hard-won freedoms" actually means, and did so in a graphic way. Violence in drama is as old as Aeschylus, sometimes as edifying as Shakespeare's *Hamlet*. With age-appropriate ratings enforced at the ticket window and the screening room, such films entertain and may even educate.

The problem is with many recent movies and lyrics that seek to glorify violence and celebrate nihilism. *Natural Born Killers* is a psychotic gross-out of a film that urges the viewer to participate in the sheer joy of slaughter. It indulges in the cruelest humor by making fun of people begging for their lives, as if pleas of fatal desperation were the antics of dispensable peasants as seen by a ruthless tyrant. This is not a mere aesthetic point. Finding grotesque humor in the desperation of people who have just learned they are about to die is exactly the response that Klebold and Harris were after as they roamed the hallways of Columbine. Nor is the "NBK" outlook a rarity. It was the culmination of a shift in American culture that can be traced back to the late 1970s with films like *Halloween* and *Friday the 13th*. Rent one of these movies and, at first, they may strike the older viewer as unusually flat—nothing "pops out at you," you can see everything coming as the killer approaches his victims in real time. That, of course, was the point. These were not meant to be thrillers. No one was meant to be surprised or put on the edge of his or her seat. These stories were simply told from the point of view of the killer—which put you in a position not of suspense, but of sensing the killer's psychotic joy in slashing hapless teens to death.

What passes for humor in today's Hollywood is also coarsening the sensibilities of our children. Making fun of the handicapped or the retarded used to be taboo in Hollywood (the rest of us called it simple decency). Now you can go to a Tom Green or Keenen Ivory Wayans movie and see for yourself that there is, in fact, a reason why taboos exist.

You can take these objections to a Hollywood insider. And the response you get back is formulaic: We have a rating system. Children are excluded from seeing this trash.

Do you buy that?

Consider what happened when federal investigators looked into this. "Companies in the entertainment industry routinely undercut their own rating restrictions by target marketing violent films, records, and video games to young audiences," said Robert Pitofsky, head of the Federal Trade Commission under President Clinton.

When the FTC studied forty-four movies rated "R" for violence, it found that thirty-five of them were targeted to children under seventeen. Marketing plans for twenty-eight of those movies, or 64 percent, contained explicit statements that the target audience included children under seventeen. Some of the other plans for these films mentioned promoting them in high schools or teen publications.

It's the same thing with music. Of fifty-five recordings with explicit content labels, the FTC found that all were targeted to children under seventeen.

Does it surprise you that among electronic games with "Mature" ratings for violence, 60 out of 118 explicitly included children under seventeen in their marketing plans? A total of eighty-three, or 70 percent, were targeted at children under seventeen.

What about the retailers' responsibility? The FTC found that just under half of movie theaters investigated admitted children ages thirteen to sixteen to R-rated films, even when not accompanied by an adult. It also found that 95 percent of the time, retailers failed to turn away unaccompanied children, ages thirteen to sixteen, when they sought explicit recordings or "Mature" electronic games.[8]

Point all this out to Hollywood insiders, and they move to the next line of defense: "C'mon, kids are smarter than you think. They recognize irony, they can separate fantasy from reality."

But can they? Consider the words of Dr. Daniel B. Borenstein, former president of the American Psychiatric Association, who told Congress, "As a nation, we are awash in a tidal wave of electronic violence.... What goes into a child's mind is just as important as what goes into a child's stomach."[9]

And just as too many of our children are living on high-sugar, high-fat diets, so too are they fed a constant and daily dose of violence. In a joint statement on the impact of entertainment violence on children, six prominent U.S. medical groups warned of the connection between media violence and violent behavior in children. The average American child spends twenty-eight hours a week watching TV and at least an hour a day playing video games and listening to rock music.

Well over a thousand studies—from the National Institute on Mental Health to the office of the U.S. Surgeon General—consistently show a link between exposure to violence in media and violent behavior in children.[10] Some children are more easily influenced than others. The effect varies with the duration and intensity of exposure. But the effect is real.

The medical groups found:

• Children who see a lot of violence are more likely to view violence as an acceptable means of resolving conflicts.

• Extended viewing of violence leads to emotional desensitizing toward violence in real life.

• Entertainment violence feeds the perception that the world is a violent and mean place. This increases aggressive self-protective behavior in children.

• Viewing violence may lead to real-life violence. Children exposed to entertainment violence have a higher tendency for violent behavior than those who are not exposed.[11]

"The correlation between violent media and aggression is larger than the effect that wearing a condom has on decreasing the risk of HIV," says Brad Bushman, a professor of psychology at Iowa State University at Ames. "It's larger than the correlation between exposure to lead and decreased IQ levels in kids. It's larger than the effects of exposure to asbestos. It's larger than the effect of secondhand smoke on cancer."[12]

A study published in *Science* that tracked seven hundred young people over seventeen years found that teenagers who watch even as little as an hour of television a day are more likely to get into fights, commit assaults, or engage in other types of violence later in life. The more television people watch, the more likely, it appears, that they will later become violent.[13]

When cornered by all this evidence, Hollywood always retreats to the argument of last resort—hands off my freedom of speech! Call for greater responsibility from artists in exercising their freedom of expression and you will be greeted with howls of "censorship."

Of course, responsibility is what America is asking for—not government censorship. Ironically, the same people who are so quick to wrap themselves and their industry in the First Amendment—who will tolerate no infringement of their right to free speech—are the most vocal in seeking infringements of the Second Amendment. Another irony, of course, is that what Hollywood despises as the "gun culture" is known by other names in heartland America—as hunting, as marksmanship, as sportsmanship, as tradition and heritage.

Young people who learn about firearms and their legitimate uses from family members, who own their guns legally, have lower rates of delinquency than those who do not own firearms, as the Department of Justice determined in a 1995 report. Go to rural America and you will also find lower rates of murder and violent crime than in urban areas—certainly lower than in Studio City, Burbank, and Hollywood. A healthy "gun culture" teaches children respect for firearms and personal responsibility.

Why, then, does Hollywood go so far out of its way to demonize peaceful people and heartland culture? There is really only one possible reason. In psychiatric circles it is known as "projection"— imagining that one's own failings belong to someone else.

They know the degree of their responsibility, but they just can't admit it.

In their hearts, they know the depth of their guilt.

Chapter Ten

Little Acorns and Bad Treaties

...there are a number of areas very explicitly set forth that could very well be used to directly involve the United Nations in domestic firearms diplomacy.

—*Congressman Bob Barr*

Imagine a "blind test" in which a gun-control activist is asked to grade unnamed countries by their willingness to enact and enforce strict gun-control laws. Then turn the card to reveal the names of the chosen countries. This little thought experiment is telling because many of the countries most eager to control firearms also rank among the most repressive.

At the top of the chart would be President Bush's "axis of evil"—North Korea, Iran, and Iraq. Fidel Castro's Cuba would also be at the top of that list.

Unfortunately, there would also be many democratic countries, like Australia, Britain, and Canada, that have recently bargained away ancient rights of individual self-defense. Now the same movement that brought gun control to these democracies has gone international. It is using world politics, the United Nations, and international treaties to do what it cannot achieve at home, to breach the last great bastion of gun rights—the United States and our Second Amendment.

Leading this international movement is a plethora of nongovernmental organizations, or NGOs, that agitate in favor of gun control. What is an NGO? It is any nonprofit, activist organization. The National Rifle Association is one kind of NGO. So are the AARP, the Sierra Club, and Mothers Against Drunk Driving. NGOs play an important role in democracies. They organize people around issues and amplify our voices through collective action.

The NRA, for example, consistently ranks among the most powerful NGOs. We achieve this not by having the best lobbyists, but because we speak for America's ninety million gun owners, twenty million hunters, and our four million dues-paying members. These people, spread out in key congressional districts throughout the country, are the source of our power.

It is one thing, however, for NGOs to participate in the democratic process. It is quite something else for them to join with international institutions to circumvent the process. In recent years, international organizations have tried to do just that—an "end run" around American democracy—by working hand in glove with NGOs. From the chambers of the United Nations, they are trying to force gun control on the United States "from the top, down."

You would think that protests against the NRA would take place at our headquarters or somewhere in the nation's capital in Washington, D.C. But it was before the United Nations on a summer day in 2001 that a group of gun controllers chanted, "NRA is not the USA." At this "Guns Know No Borders" rally, protestors trotted out for the cameras a puppet effigy of President Bush, depicting him as a marionette of the gun industry. An Amnesty International USA official was on hand to underscore that gun control is now "a human rights issue." Lora Lumpe of the Norwegian Initiative on Small Arms Transfers said, "This issue is too important to allow timid government leaders to block progress. That is why popular, community movements from Liberia, Brazil, Kenya, Honduras, Philippines, Cambodia, South Africa, and Russia joined their allies from inside

the United States in a rally to stop gun trafficking and save lives."
These countries, of course, would save many more lives if they
focused on fighting crime at home and helped their citizens defend
themselves from criminal predators.

Also on hand for the antigun rally were the usual, dependable fellow travelers of the Left, the Children's Defense Fund, the Brady
Campaign, and the ever-present Physicians for Social Responsibility.[1] Their contribution? To link civil wars in other countries to—you
guessed it—the nonexistent "gun-show loophole." Not only are
American gun shows now portrayed as the armory of world terrorism, in their view, but the gun show in Reno, Boise, or Des Moines
is also supposedly feeding wars in Colombia, Liberia, and Sudan.

This connection between gun shows in American suburbs and
civil strife in distant lands is absurd on its face. A more serious question has to do with the real cause of the general level of social violence. What about the link between gun laws and crime rates in
different countries?

Democracies in Peril

International studies show no connection between restrictive gun
control and lower levels of crime. The reverse is actually the case.
After surveying twenty-seven countries, congressional researchers
reported, "It is difficult to find a correlation between the existence
of strict firearms regulations and a lower incidence of gun-related
crimes." Canada cracked down on handguns and suffered a dramatic
increase in the percentage of homicides caused by handguns.
Researchers found higher crime in strictly regulated Germany than
in countries with liberal gun policies like Israel and Switzerland.[2]

Where does the United States fit into all of this? The brutal truth
is that guns or no guns, the United States ranks as a violent country
among developed nations. Cathy Young, a writer in Boston, reported:
"Even if we had somehow gotten rid not only of handguns but of all
guns, and even if, improbably, none of the killers who used guns
would have substituted some other weapon, we still would have been

left with 2.1 murders for every 100,000 people—about four times the average annual homicide rate in Japan (0.5 per 100,000) and higher than the homicide rates in Great Britain (1.2) or Sweden (1.4)."

She went on to note that Switzerland, boasting "a heavily armed population and a thriving gun culture (shooting contests for children are a popular tradition)," has a homicide rate comparable to Great Britain's. Armed-to-the-teeth Israel, with most adults on active duty or in the reserves, also has a low murder rate comparable to Britain's.

What about suicide? Young reports that the 1996 suicide rate in the United States was 11.8 per 100,000. In gun-restrictive Canada it was 13.4, in Japan it was 17.9, in France it was 20.9, and in Finland it was 25.[3]

Obviously, social pathology—not guns—determines how violent a society will be. The sad truth is that many developed democracies have not only traded away their gun rights for dubious benefit—they have also given up their traditions and abrogated the civil rights of their people to a shocking degree.

When one considers the "ABC" countries of Australia, Britain, and Canada, one finds a consistent pattern—that of old-line democracies beginning to turn their backs on ancient traditions that began with the Magna Carta, in the lame attempt to scapegoat their failed domestic policy initiatives onto the very freedoms they are built upon.

Great Britain: Philip Bourjaily, writing in the pages of the *American Rifleman*, tells how both Rudyard Kipling and Arthur Conan Doyle were startled by the skill with which Boer farmer-riflemen were able to rain lethal fire down on British troops during the Boer War in 1899. As a result, both writers returned to England determined to promote civilian marksmanship through the expansion of rifle clubs. By the First World War, Britain boasted some 1,900 rifle clubs.[4]

Alas, we know all too well what happened next. In between the World Wars, Britain reversed its policy of encouraging private ownership of rifles. Restrictive laws took their toll, reducing rifle clubs to only 471. Licenses have been required for rifles and handguns since 1920, and for shotguns since 1967. A decade ago semi-automatic and pump-action center-fire rifles, and all handguns except single-shot .22s, were prohibited. The .22s were banned in 1997. Shotguns must be registered, and semi-automatic shotguns that can hold more than two shells must be licensed.

Despite tight licensing procedures in recent years, handgun-related robbery in Britain rose 200 percent during the last dozen years, five times as fast as the rise in the United States. While Britain's tight handgun laws have not been able to reverse a crime wave, this mother country of ancient liberties is methodically shedding the democratic rights of its citizenry. Britain today places strict qualifications on freedom of speech and the right to assemble, allowing, for example, book bans, censorship of videos, and prior restraint of speech. Lacking the equivalent of a Supreme Court to strike down unconstitutional laws, Parliament is increasingly giving police more power to stop and search vehicles as well as pedestrians. Civil jury trials in Great Britain have been abolished in all cases except libel; criminal jury trials are rare. Police are allowed to continue to interrogate suspects who have asked that the interrogation be halted. They are also allowed to keep defense lawyers away from suspects under interrogation for limited periods. Evidence derived from a coerced confession is allowed.

Has this curtailment of democratic traditions made Britons safer? A June 2000 *CBS Evening News* report proclaimed Great Britain "one of the most violent urban societies in the Western world." Dan Rather declared, "This summer, thousands of Americans will travel to Britain expecting a civilized island free from crime and ugliness.... [But now] the U.K. has a crime problem...worse than ours."[5]

Canada: Handguns were registered in 1934. A 1977 law eliminated protection of property as a reason for acquiring a handgun, and required registration of "restricted weapons," including semi-

automatic rifles. The notorious 1995 Canadian Firearms Act prohibited compact handguns and all handguns in .32 or .25 caliber—
half of privately owned handguns. It required all gun owners to be
licensed by January 1, 2000, and to register all rifles and shotguns by
January 1, 2003. Following the British example, this law granted the
police powers of "search and seizure," allowing them to enter homes
without search warrants, to inspect gun storage procedures, and to
look for unregistered guns.

Because Canada has no Fifth Amendment, suspected gun owners
in that country can be forced to testify against themselves. Illegally
seized evidence is admissible in court, while security services maintain files on one out of every forty Canadians. Have these policies
worked? From 1978 to 1988, Canada's burglary rate increased
25 percent, surpassing the U.S. rate. Half of burglaries in Canada
occur in occupied homes, compared to about 10 to 13 percent in the
United States. Studies done a few decades ago show that ethnically
and economically similar areas of the United States and Canada had
virtually identical homicide rates, despite significantly different
firearm laws.[6]

Australia: Licensing of gun owners was imposed in 1973, registration of firearms was imposed in 1985, and in 1996 semi-automatic
center-fire rifles and many semi-automatic and pump-action shotguns were prohibited. By 2000, Australian authorities had confiscated some 660,000 privately owned firearms for destruction. Once
again, we see gun control moving hand-in-hand with a rise in crime.
The Australian Institute of Criminology reports that between 1996
and 1998 assaults rose 16 percent, armed robberies rose 73 percent,
and unlawful entries rose 8 percent.

What has prompted the "ABC" countries to infringe on civil liberties that once made them democratic exemplars of the world? A
futile and self-defeating move toward the illusion of perfect safety.
The worst trend in the "ABC" countries is the declining respect for
the principle of self-defense, a trend seen in the rising prosecutions

of people in Britain and Canada who used guns for purely defensive reasons.

Perhaps you find all this talk about the abrogation of our Anglo-Saxon heritage off-topic. The point is, it doesn't matter if you're of African, Latino, or Asian descent—whatever your ethnic background, the Anglo-Saxon tradition of respect for the rights of the individual is a precious inheritance for all peoples, for all time. It is disturbing, then, and not a little ironic, to see the extent to which these hallowed traditions are no longer practiced by Anglo-Saxons themselves.

There are even more disturbing compromises being made in other democracies. Consider two, Germany and Japan.[7]

Germany: German gun laws are about as restrictive as those proposed by U.S. gun-control advocates—in short, they could scarcely be more restrictive. Yet, predictably, the annual number of firearm-related murders in Germany is rising (it jumped 76 percent between 1992 and 1995). The German people, with some of the world's most stringent controls on guns, were shocked to suffer a Columbine-style school shooting that left seventeen dead in the small city of Erfurt in May 2002.[8]

The unfortunate response of the central government was to—you guessed it—pass even more gun laws!

Japan: This consensus-driven society may be the only one in the world in which gun control has actually coincided with low crime. However, the price the Japanese pay in terms of a loss of civil liberties is quite high. Japanese police routinely search citizens at will, and twice a year inspect residences. Suspects can be detained without bail for twenty-eight days before being arraigned before a judge. The confession rate is 95 percent, the trial conviction rate is 99.91 percent. Defendants have no right to a jury. Amnesty International has called Japan's police custody system a "flagrant violation of United Nations human rights principles." Even the Tokyo Bar Association charges that Japanese police "engage in torture or illegal treatment."

Attorney David Kopel sums up the state of world affairs in his book *The Samurai, the Mountie, and the Cowboy*: "Despite strict and sometimes Draconian gun controls in other nations, guns remain readily available on the criminal black market. . . . The experiences of [England, Japan, Canada, and the United States] point to social control as far more important than gun control. Gun control validates other authoritarian features of the society. Exaltation of the police and submission to authority are values, which, when internally adopted by the citizenry, keep people out of trouble with the law. The most important effect of gun control in Japan and the Commonwealth is that it reinforces the message that citizens must be obedient to the government."[9]

Grandstanding at the UN

How can the United Nations possibly impose gun control on the United States? It cannot—unless the U.S. Senate ratifies an international treaty to that effect.

What the UN *can* do is stigmatize U.S. gun laws, giving Eurocrats and the rest of the silk-stocking diplomatic set another chance to denounce the "unilateralism" of America for sticking to our guns. This, in turn, gives domestic gun controllers a propaganda point— America's stand on guns is isolating us from the rest of the world!

Like a third-rate mystery, the UN initiative began in Cairo. At that time, Japan led an effort at the Ninth United Nations Congress on the Prevention of Crime and the Treatment of Offenders to "promote the adequate control of firearms" with a "common strategy for effective control of firearms at the global level." The Japanese went on to propose a ban on handguns by anyone except police and target shooters—with target shooters required to lock away their guns at the range. The Japanese representative called for universal firearms licensing and centralized computer registration, adding that "citizens should not need to possess handguns for self-defense."

How one wishes that a U.S. diplomat had had the pluck to introduce a motion to "examine the denial of basic procedural rights and the torture of suspects by police in major developed countries that begin with a J." These being the Clinton years, however, our U.S. representatives sat on their hands, giving these proceedings their silent approval.

Naturally, this would not be an international "congress" worthy of the name if delegates did not call for an international study. Of the eleven experts appointed to the study, two came from Japan and three from Canada (including one from the Canadian Justice Department official's "International Firearms Centre" who had been deeply involved in the passage of Canada's universal gun-registration bill).

U.S. officials continued to sit by in silence when, in the May 1996 UN Commission on Crime Prevention and Criminal Justice, speaker after speaker called for the internationalization of gun control.[10]

If you follow politics at all, you know a lot of people in Washington, D.C., want to take away your right to keep and bear arms. The truth is they have the whole world on their side, because the systematic disarming of a free people is happening across the globe today. From around the world, the message is clear—your guns are next. Only one thing stands in their way, the Second Amendment and the NRA.

—Charlton Heston

By 2001, international bureaucrats were ready to make their move with a treaty that would ban the transfer of small arms to "nonstate actors"—in other words, everyone but recognized government authorities. The proposal would have sailed through except for one thing—reality was going off-script, for Al Gore had not become president. The U.S. negotiators sent to New York were picked by President George W. Bush—and they took a dim view of any move to curtail the Second Amendment.

"You can have good and bad nonstate actors," one U.S. official told the *Washington Times*. "Would you want to keep weapons from the French Resistance in World War II? You wouldn't be able to sell weapons to them...or any resistance group opposing genocide."[11]

Read literally, the measure would seem to outlaw the supply of arms to the beleaguered Kurds of Iraq, or perhaps the state of Israel. U.S. representatives noted that the terms of the treaty might even rule out sending arms to Taiwan.

Even worse, the treaty's language on weapons of military design was incredibly overbroad. The definition of small arms in the draft treaty covered just about every hunting rifle in the world, as well as revolvers. There were other disturbing proposals—including language that could potentially define just about every gun dealer in the world as a "gun trafficker."

The good news is that while gun-control fanatics held their angry, effigy-ridden rallies outside, U.S. negotiators had a lot of support on the inside. The World Forum ably represented an international coalition of thirty gun-rights groups, including the National Rifle Association.[12]

As this measure lurched toward ratification, a number of Second Amendment leaders went to the United Nations to make sure nothing passed that would compromise our rights. Among them was Congressman Bob Barr of Georgia, a constant and alert presence at the proceedings.

For anyone inclined to imagine that elections don't matter and that U.S. politicians are all the same, take note of the excellent representation our diplomats were offering by 2001.

John R. Bolton, U.S. undersecretary of state for arms control, bluntly warned delegates that we would not allow the United Nations to dictate our domestic policies. "The United States believes that the responsible use of firearms is a legitimate aspect of national life," he said. "Like many countries, the United States has a cultural tradition of hunting and sport shooting."[13]

Americans, he said, do not find all guns "problematic."

And with that warning shot across the bow, he proceeded to pressure the delegates to remove any part of the measure that could threaten the Second Amendment. While the UN passed measures strictly to reduce the flow of arms into conflict zones, U.S. negotiators

• succeeded in removing any language that could halt the sale of weapons to foreign militias, in order to maintain the ability to arm groups fighting genocidal regimes;

• rejected any limits on the civilian ownership of guns;

• discarded language that would define civilian guns as "military-style weapons."

Still, UN delegates, worn out after a night of negotiations, bitterly complained about the way in which they were forced to buckle to the "concerns of one state." Among those expressing their disappointment were delegates from China, Cuba, Vietnam, Egypt, and Mali.[14]

The *New York Times*, in high dudgeon, sniffed, "The Bush administration might as well have sent Charlton Heston ... to deliver its opening address to a United Nations conference on small arms earlier this week."[15]

Undersecretary Bolton, however, had the final word. He showed recognition of the nature of the threat of seemingly innocuous moves. "From little acorns," he said, "bad treaties grow."[16]

And, we might add, it is from little acorns like these that a country like the United States can easily grow into an Australia, a Britain, or a Canada.

Chapter Eleven

Gun Control and "Silver Bullets"

If Americans believed in political correctness, we'd still be King George's boys—subjects bound to the British crown.

—*Charlton Heston, in an address to Harvard Law School students*

Politics is about passion and votes.

That is why the NRA ranked number one in *Fortune* magazine's survey of groups that have the most clout in Washington, D.C.[1]

We're not the nation's largest lobby, not by far—the AARP has 31 million more members than we do. Nor does our clout come from our treasure chest. It comes from the absolute commitment of our members—those who "get it," who see through the veil of big media untruths. Our strength comes from Americans who understand that this debate over guns is not over technicalities, but over freedom.

Ultimately, passion always wins the day. People impassioned by a cause take the time to vote. They pass along information to family members or friends who are misled or confused by media distortions. They support the NRA. They may not wear their pride on their sleeves, but they proudly proclaim their membership on the bumpers of their cars and trucks.

The NRA wins most of the time because we know that when we sound an alarm, the American heartland will mobilize.

Mobilize against the candidates of gun control.

Mobilize against the referendums of gun control.

Mobilize against the Trojan Horse issues of illusory safety.

One thing, however, we do not do is mobilize one party against the other. Though many have painted us as a wing of the Republican Party, we are in truth a nonpartisan organization. Over the years, millions of Democrats have supported the NRA, and we have supported them. We have counted among our leaders and friends stalwarts of the Democratic Party like Congressman John Dingell of Michigan. At the same time, many liberal Republicans—and some ill-informed Beltway conservatives with knee-jerk reactions—rank among our worst adversaries as strident advocates of gun control.

At a recent national convention, we had a very special keynote speaker, Zell Miller of Georgia. Once a governor of Georgia, now a U.S. senator—and always a U.S. Marine—Zell is a leading Democrat who spoke with great passion about gun ownership and what it means to him. Hearing one of the nation's leading Democrats make an impassioned plea for Second Amendment freedom was one of the most striking moments since our election victories in 2000. (You can read his remarks in full in the Appendix at the back of this book.)

Senator Miller proves that the presumed gulf between the NRA and the party that once was home to two gun collectors named Jefferson and Jackson was unnatural. He no doubt remembers that the greatest Democrat of modern times, Franklin Delano Roosevelt, used to bounce his car through Georgia fields to catch a coon in the headlights for his hunter friends. Throughout the 1990s, however, the Clinton-Gore administration led the national Democratic Party deep into an unthinking, ideological commitment against hallowed American traditions. The Clinton-Gore operatives were convinced that gun control was a "silver bullet" issue that would allow them to slay their Republican opponents. It took ten years of losing elections—losing the Senate, losing the House, losing the White House—to convince most Democrats to remove gun control from their agendas. The story of that struggle is worth retelling, because it shows how powerful and determined Second Amendment detractors can be—and where they are going next.

And it shows just how powerful our members can be when our families and communities are insulted, our way of life disparaged, and our basic values and freedoms threatened.

The Bigotry of the Blue

Paul Begala, former Clinton-Gore advisor, now political operative and media commentator, really let the cat out of the bag when he vented his feelings about the last election in an Internet column: "What is it about peace and prosperity that has them so angry? Could it be that the Clinton administration was the first in history to take on the extremists at the NRA?"

He pointed to the famous *USA Today* electoral map that showed Bush counties in red and Gore counties in blue, saying, "But if you look closely at that map...you see the state [Texas] where James Byrd was lynch-dragged behind a pickup truck until his body came apart—it's red.... You see the state [Oklahoma] where right-wing extremists blew up a federal office building and murdered scores of federal employees—it's red...."

Never mind the irony that it is the blue concentrations—the big cities of the East and West Coasts—that mark the centers of criminal violence in America. Begala's rant was not about crime. It was, as Peggy Noonan noted, "hatred pure and simple."

Statements like these don't, if you'll forgive the pun, just come out of the blue. Gross, negative stereotypes of hunters and the "gun culture" have long been tossed around by liberal elites. Typical of this kind of bigotry was a remark tossed out by former New York governor Mario Cuomo, who famously characterized gun owners as "hunters who drink beer, don't vote, and lie to their wives about where they were all weekend."[2]

Imagine the media uproar if he had said that about any other group in America. As it turns out, gun owners noticed and took deep offense. Cuomo seemed not to have grasped that parts of upstate New York are as wedded to hunting traditions as the American West, and that their traditions hark back all the way to the scenes depicted by James Fenimore Cooper. To his surprise, Cuomo was eventually tossed out of office.

The statements of Begala and Cuomo reveal a deep-seated aversion to much of the quintessential American ideal. This aversion was on display in the 2000 presidential election, and goes far in explaining why after eight years of peace and prosperity under a Democratic president, the election landed on a dime's edge.

Election 2000: Power Play

By the time the Democrats had nominated Al Gore for the White House, respected national Democratic pollsters had convinced themselves that gun control was a winning issue that would separate suburbanites and women from "angry white men" who would never vote for a liberal candidate. Among them was Peter Hart, who advised clients that he had never seen a climate as favorable to gun control as that of August 2000—with skewed polls showing gun restrictions running just behind education and the economy as voters' top priorities.[3]

And so the party of Jefferson and Jackson went on an all-out offensive to tear down the Second Amendment. There was no beating around the bush about it either. The antigun movement became solidly partisan, as much a part of the Democratic Party as the trial lawyers. "My friend, if you and I truly want a safer America, we cannot allow George W. Bush to be elected president of the United States," Sarah Brady wrote in a fundraising letter. "A political disaster of that magnitude would mean four long years of being on the defensive."[4]

Many Democratic candidates went against the grain of previous elections and came out hard for gun control, even in Western states with deep and sentimental attachments to pioneer traditions. They were attempting what political analysts call a paradigm shift, trying to rearrange the very landscape of American politics.

Even "President Bartlet" from NBC's *West Wing* jumped into the act, with Martin Sheen appearing in gun-control ads that ran in Cleveland, Detroit, Kansas City, Milwaukee, Philadelphia, St. Louis, Toledo, and West Palm Beach.[5]

A Republican candidate for the Senate, George F. Allen, found himself in the crosshairs. At the eleventh hour, Virginia voters began to receive recorded phone calls in which a woman, saying her son had been killed by "gun violence," squarely put the blame for this crime at Allen's feet. Among the backers of these calls was George Soros, as well as a liberal movie producer. Even more disgusting were calls that went to African-American voters claiming that Allen kept a noose in his law office, insinuating that he was in favor of lynching, and implying that he was a racist for keeping a Confederate flag at his home. Union workers in Virginia mines received calls telling them that the Republicans were out to cut their pensions.[6]

Virginia voters were not so easily fooled. Allen went to the Senate.

The same held for the top of the ticket. Al Gore, who had so strongly come out for extending Washington, D.C.–style gun control to all of America in the wake of the National Zoo shootings, belatedly recognized the cost of gun control. Tracking polls showed him even with Bush in the Clinton-Gore home states of Arkansas and Tennessee—two states he should have been winning handily. At the last minute, Gore tried to trim his sails and began speaking in warmer tones about the importance of hunting in his mythical youth. He started to make pro-gun noises before union audiences.

Gore had finally grasped the magnitude of his mistake, but it was too little, too late.

The national Democrats thought they were driving a wedge in the heart of the opposition. In truth, they were driving a stake into their own hearts. They never stopped to appreciate the nature of their own "base," their most solid and loyal supporters. Polls taken in the mid-1990s showed that almost one in four voters who identified themselves as liberals owned a gun. Among voters who identified themselves as Democrats, the ratio was even higher—one in three.[7]

Just as Democrats lost the House of Representatives in 1994, in part over the gun issue (a fact that President Clinton implicitly acknowledged), so did Al Gore pay a terrible price for eight years of agitating for gun control. Again, Arkansas and Tennessee—the latter the very state Al Gore had represented as a U.S. senator—turned out to be keys to a Bush victory, as did West Virginia, usually reliable for the Democrats. Gore was particularly hurt by the defection of the labor-union vote in these particular states. While union households traditionally back Democrats in presidential elections (they chose Bill Clinton over Bob Dole by a 2-1 margin), in 2000 the labor vote was equally split between Bush and Gore. Had Gore won a few thousand more votes in Arkansas, Tennessee, or West Virginia, he would be president today.

Not only had the Democrats lost the presidency by a cellophane-thin margin, they had squandered an excellent chance to retake the House as well.

House Democratic leader Richard Gephardt of Missouri recounted for the media his astonished reaction to the attitude of voters: "I go door-to-door in my district, still do today, all the time. And I had a man come to the door. He said, 'I like you. I'm with you on all the issues, but I'm going to vote against you this time.' I said, 'Why?' He said, 'You want to take my gun away.'"[8]

While the bottom dropped out among traditional Democratic constituencies, pro-gun voters came out in force. Exit polls showed that a full 48 percent of Americans who voted kept a gun in the house.[9] A Roper Starch Worldwide survey found that 93 percent of hunters who are registered to vote did vote—and they cast their votes for Bush in near-monolithic numbers.[10]

Charlie Cook, master political analyst, said: "The NRA did a phenomenal job....I think Democrats need to do a lot of real hard thinking about what they are going to do on guns, because it's a tough choice. Because, in effect, it writes off rural and small town voters and a segment of unionist voters."[11] That sentiment was echoed by the AFL-CIO's national political director, Steve Rosenthal, who urged Democrats to stop talking about gun control, otherwise they will continue to see an erosion in their support from union members.

Even Bill Clinton had to acknowledge the obvious in a TV interview: "[The NRA has] probably had more to do than anyone else with the fact that we didn't win the House this time. And they hurt Al Gore."[12]

We think it hurts our party's message in rural areas to have our party leaders advocating further gun control. I think you will see less advocacy by the leadership on the Democratic side of any gun-control proposals because of our concerns.   —Congressman Jim Turner, Texas Democrat

Backtracking

Stan Greenberg, a leading Democratic pollster, is now advising his clients to put less emphasis on gun control. He hardly needs to give that advice. In 1994, 1996, and 2000, congressional Democrats placed their bets on gun control. Now, after many losses and close shaves, it should be clear to all that when it comes to explicit gun control, this dog not only won't hunt, it won't even lift up its head.

Newsweek has reported that Bush aides "practically dare" the Democrats to make the so-called gun-show loophole an issue in this election. "Most of the key Senate races are in rural states," one strategist said. "You think the Democrats will want to make a big deal of the gun-show loophole in, say, Georgia?"[13]

"I think people felt burned by 2000 on the gun issue," Greenberg said. "I don't see any pressure to get the gun issue on the national agenda. I don't even see a discussion of it. It's not even that they're debating it and deciding against it. I think it's just taken for granted that it's not going to be emphasized."

James Carville, the "ragin' Cajun" defender of Bill Clinton, said, "I don't think there's a Second Amendment right to own a gun. But I think it's a loser political issue."[14]

The never-ending tendency of government to aggregate more power and control over our lives remains—as do the thousands of bureaucrats who were the line workers of the Clinton-Gore gun-control machine. We are just getting started on reversing eight years of sweeping attacks on our rights— and it is simply the nature of government that what has been done is ten times harder to undo.

—James Jay Baker

Read Greenberg and Carville carefully, though, and you'll see that they haven't changed their spots—they've just painted them over. Many big-city Democrats—and, for that matter, some "moderate" Republicans—remain as committed as ever to the idea of gun control. They haven't relinquished one iota of ideology, but they have changed their color. To paraphrase Samuel Johnson, the prospect of political annihilation concentrates the mind wonderfully.

The best example of this is Tom Strickland of Colorado. In 1996 when Democrat Strickland went up against Republican Wayne Allard for a seat in the U.S. Senate, campaign supporters sent out thousands of brochures with dramatic photos of burial services and a blunt headline: "How many more will die before Wayne Allard votes to ban assault weapons?" Allard was a ranch-raised veterinarian who stood by the Second Amendment. To the Democrats' everlasting shock, the only burial service to result from that brochure was the one that entombed Strickland's 1996 electoral ambitions. The people of Colorado saw through this weak attempt at fear-mongering and deliberate distortion. They voted for Allard.

So what is Strickland doing in the 2002 campaign? He is taking on Senator Allard as—you guessed it—an avid hunter.

"We don't need any more gun control," he says. "You just need to enforce the laws you already have." Strickland rhapsodizes about shooting deer as a youth and pheasants as an adult. But he's not going all the way to the center. Strickland's true colors still show in his criticism of Senator Allard for trying to repeal the ban on myth-ical "assault weapons." He still harps on Senator Allard's "100 per-cent NRA voting record."[15]

As Tom Strickland shows, the pro-gun forces have retrenched, not gone away. The gun-control lobbies are willing to give candidates like Strickland room for a bit of distancing. Recognizing their losses at the polls, they are also redoubling their efforts at gun control by other routes. In some states, this may take the form of electing or appoint-ing liberal activist judges willing to legislate from the bench. In other states, they are seeking to enact gun control through the initiative and referendum process that is a populist feature of Western politics.

Andrew McKelvey's Americans for Gun Safety (AGS) is at the heart of this new national movement. AGS has strengthened its national organization, hiring consultants to work the media in every state (and in some cases, executing a wholesale takeover of chapters of less sophisticated gun-control operations). Measures to close the (nonexistent) "gun-show loophole" are popular causes among gun-control groups. Two such measures—lavishly funded by wealthy individuals and bolstered by slick, packaged appeals—passed as bal-lot measures in Colorado and Oregon.

These are cash-rich efforts funded by plutocrats. The Colorado measure, Amendment 22, was swamped by $500,000 in spending by AGS on ads featuring Senator McCain.[16] In fact, total AGS spend-ing in that election cycle came close to $3 million.[17] An affiliated organization, SAFE Colorado, funded by big contributors that included Rosie O'Donnell, hit the million-dollar mark.[18] Handgun Control, Inc., and its PAC invested $5 million for gun-control mea-sures in several states.[19]

While Tom Strickland goes about Colorado doing a weak Charl-ton Heston imitation, AGS is spending small fortunes on radio ads linking Allard to the phony gun-show issue. AGS insists that it is not trying to defeat Allard, just get his attention.

History is clear. If AGS keeps it up in Colorado, Allard will be reelected handily.[20]

Blue Dogs *Can* Hunt

While many Democrats are undertaking a patently insincere approach on gun control, others are emerging as genuine leaders of Second Amendment rights. They mostly come from the conservative wing of the Democratic Party, often described as "Blue Dog Democrats." Though a minority in their party, they occupy a pivotal place in the House of Representatives, an independent swing vote of conscience.

The philosophy of these Democrats is embraced by a rare blue dog in the Senate, Zell Miller, who did far more than appear at an NRA convention. He spoke in moving and defiant tones that can only come from someone who thoroughly understands the issue, and grasps the importance of this fundamental American right.

His gut instinct told him that Democratic pollsters were misleading the party, that they were asking the wrong question in the wrong way. Senator Miller noted the results when people are asked to agree or disagree with the following statement: "Whenever I hear politicians talking about gun control, it makes me wonder if they understand my values or my way of life."

The results of these internal Democratic polls were stark. Some 73 percent of respondents agreed with that statement. This result was not an anomaly. Poll after poll confirms strong support among the American people for gun ownership, and apprehension toward those who would restrict it.

An ABCNews.com poll, taken in the spring of 2002, came up with a number identical to that of the Democrats' internal poll—73 percent. This is the majority that—after having the Second Amendment read to them over the phone—agree with the Ashcroft Justice Department position that it guarantees the right to individual gun ownership. Only 20 percent believed it guarantees only the right of states to maintain militias. What about proponents of "strong" gun control? They were at a ten-year low, 39 percent—a large minority, to be sure.

These findings are consistent with a 1998 survey by Lawrence Research that found that, by an eight-to-one majority, Americans believe we have the right to defend our homes with a handgun.[21]

Americans are as solid as ever on the basic concepts of political freedom, but at the margins they can be confused by issues deceptively named and deceptively framed in the Buzzword Factory. In shaping public opinion in the future, the major media conglomerates will remain central.

This brings us back, full circle, to McCain's "campaign finance reform" bill described in the first chapter. By restricting political speech during the crucial period leading up to an election, campaign finance "reform" ensures that the only voice we will hear will be those of well-funded incumbents and powerful media conglomerates.

Think back to that red and blue map.

This new law gives a monopoly to the media cartels that broadcast from the pockets of blue, to tell those of us in the red all we need to know about politics.

The enemies of our political freedoms are as restless and relentless as ever.

In domestic policy, no less than in foreign policy, eternal vigilance is the price of freedom.

Conclusion

If Canada can do it ... if Australia can do it ... if England can
do it ... we can do it!
  —Marion Wright Edelman at the Million Mom March rally

Guard with jealous attention the public liberty. Suspect everyone who approaches that jewel.
             —Patrick Henry

One man was in the air, the other had his feet planted firmly on
the ground. One was middle-aged, the other elderly. One faced
sophisticated international terrorists, the other a common bumbler
turned psychopath. But when it came time to act, both Tom Burnett
on United Flight 93 and Al Gratia in Luby's cafeteria said the same
thing as they rose up out of their seats.

The last recorded words of both men expressed a determination
to "do something." When faced by monsters who believe they can
win our respect by making us afraid, Americans have always acted
this way. From the Boston Massacre to Pearl Harbor, Americans
have always had to *do something*.

This is the spirit of those who took our fight to Afghanistan and
won. This is the spirit of a humble nation that will yield to compas-
sion, but will never bow to coercion.

And, we would add, this same unconquerable spirit is on display
in the streets of America. Because some of us are gun owners and
gun carriers, we have turned the corner on the more pedestrian

forms of terrorism that lurk in the alleys and side streets. Just as Americans united to fight terror, so have large numbers of us united in the majority of U.S. states to allow ordinary citizens to deter crime with a right-to-carry.

Those who predicted that the streets of urban America would flow red from Wild West shootouts look pretty silly now. Right-to-carry has been one of the most conspicuous policy successes of modern times. Federal penalties for gun criminals have also worked. So has getting tough about criminals' prison sentences and parole.

Americans can easily grasp a distinction that escapes the opinion elite—gun-control laws, by their very nature, only disarm the law-abiding. Common sense for most, but rocket science to some. In his famous essay, Jeffrey Snyder identified the common fallacy shared by intellectuals of both conservative and liberal stripes. They have an abounding faith in the power of the word, an overestimation of the power of the rights set forth in the First Amendment, and a general disregard for the virtue of action.

"Implicit in calls for the repeal of the Second Amendment is the assumption that our First Amendment rights are sufficient to preserve our liberty," he wrote. "The belief is that liberty can be preserved as long as men freely speak their minds; that there is no tyranny or abuse that can survive being exposed in the press; and that the truth need only be disclosed for the culprits to be shamed. The people will act, and the truth shall set us, and keep us, free."

Snyder gives this view thorough consideration, then concludes: "History is not kind to this belief. Only people willing and able to defend themselves can preserve their liberties."[1]

Canada, the European Union, and Japan are increasingly betting their security and freedoms on the hope that everyone will respect their stringent rule making. Alone among the major nations, Americans instinctively grasp that the only rules that are universally respected are the rules of physics.

We may wish this weren't so. We may wish that civilization were so advanced that the deterrent threat of force would never be necessary. But we cannot wish away the world into which we were born—a world in which some people cannot be reasoned with.

Americans have chosen to act in a spirit of realism by taking back our streets and taking back our rights. No wonder right-to-carry is so alarming to the utopians among us. States with concealed-carry laws have been so successful at reducing crime and violence that they deeply threaten the whole premise of the gun-control lobby. And when the gun controllers have tried to take this success head-on, to reverse America's thinking, that lobby has lost election after election. Entirely too much freedom is breaking out, all over—and so the champions of control are beginning to panic.

Like any political force on the losing end of a debate, the gun-control lobby has resorted to its old standby tactics—sowing fear and confusion. They are now trying to make Americans believe that gun issues are somehow related to terrorism. They are trying to make Americans believe that determined international terrorists are drawn to our shores to attend gun shows and exploit a nonexistent "loophole."

This may sound silly, but this message—put in the skillful hands of the best advertising people on Madison Avenue, guided by the sharpest pollsters in Washington, D.C., backed by billionaires with limitless pockets—can be made to sound convincing and real. Efforts to control gun shows, and all manner of other American traditions, will continue to swarm out of the hive of activism that we've examined throughout this book.

Hollywood will continue to demonize America's "gun culture" in movies and whip up media creations like the Million Mom March.

Trial lawyers will continue to probe for trap doors in civil law through which to effectively jettison the Second Amendment.

World diplomats and nongovernmental organizations will continue to stigmatize America and prod us onto the path of Australia, Britain, and Canada.

Public intellectuals will continue to write bad history, telling you that the America we were raised to revere never really existed.

Double-dealing politicians will always be talking out of both sides of their mouths. They'll tell us how much they loved in their youth to hunt quail, ducks, or doves with dear old Dad. Then they'll work behind the scenes to advance proposals—carefully packaged to sound reasonable—that will ultimately take away our gun rights.

And for every place like Florida, where we are allowed to exercise our Second Amendment rights, there is a place like Andover, Massachusetts, where you must have the written permission of a physician to own a gun. In the Andovers of America, rest assured, members of the local country club can easily obtain such letters from their golfing partners. But if you're a convenience store clerk, or a single mother, or a nurse who has to walk alone to her car at a late hour, you might not easily find an Rx for your rights.

There are always going to be Andovers, people and places where elitist thinking rules. At the national level, the forces of gun control have only to get lucky once—one major new law, one significant court ruling, one pliable president, to create the kind of America they can now only dream about. To make America itself one big Andover.

The champions of control are going to have a tremendous advantage in the years ahead if they continue to exploit America's new atmosphere of fear and uncertainty. After all, America today is at war with a phantom foe, faceless and unfixed. There is no telling how long this war will last or how it will end—if it ever truly ends.

A climate of fear has always been a field of opportunity for those who would narrow the scope of freedom. Throughout history, from ancient Greece and Rome to the dictatorships of the twentieth century, frightened peoples have eagerly offered up their freedoms in exchange for what they believed would be greater security and order.

This is a very real danger in an America that lives in constant tension between the two necessities of freedom and security. For the moment, the passion and the political momentum are on the security side of the equation. One man's "security precaution" can easily open the door for government to act against anyone or anything that happens to fall within its crosshairs.

In the years ahead, we will be pressured as never before to engage in a fire sale of freedoms in the name of safety. This temptation will come in the form of national ID cards. It will come in the form of feel-good security measures that terrorists can easily sidestep but that will allow the government to track each and every one of us. Above all, many will face the temptation to control our guns in the name of safety.

We have to ask, is it realistic to believe the Second Amendment can survive in the twenty-first century? In looking ahead, we should take confidence from two realizations. The first is that if freedom-loving Americans stand together, we will stand tall. And nowhere can you cast a longer shadow than with the National Rifle Association. The NRA is the oldest civil rights organization in the United States, and the number-one champion of freedom. We are passionate about the Bill of Rights as a whole. If you want to make that stand for freedom, then make your stand with us.

Second, we have to realize that we must be in this fight for freedom for the long haul. The effort to preserve our political freedoms is not a temporary campaign. It is a struggle that existed centuries before we were born, and will continue for as long as men and women are willing to face up to the forces of coercion and control. We must always remember that freedom isn't free.

Our commitment to freedom will endure, even in the midst of a do-nothing world of sitcom satire and music-video mindlessness. All we have to do is observe our obligation to educate ourselves and to guide ourselves.

We have an obligation to do that, to remember the Founders.

To remember the great things they said and their willingness to put their fortunes and very lives on the line for their beliefs.

To stand on our own two feet.

To question every prepackaged assumption and bit of canned outrage thrown at us by a relentlessly biased media.

To know that if we lose the ability to think for ourselves, we lose everything. These are the truths we need to grasp and hold close. And these are the truths about our national heritage of individual responsibility that we need to instill in our children and ask them to instill into the hearts and minds of succeeding generations.

We want our children to understand that America will remain exceptional for as long as Americans insist on their freedoms.

Above all, we want our children to be proud—and never ashamed—of the fact that to be an American is to be different from all the rest of the world.

Postscript

It's unfortunate, but the lively political debate about the merits of private gun ownership all too often obscures any discussion of the overwhelmingly positive influence the shooting sports have on everyday American life. Long before baseball, football, and basketball were even invented, Americans were enjoying the benefits of hunting, target shooting, and ordinary "plinking." Today, that vibrant tradition lives on, providing millions of Americans with safe, affordable, and family-friendly recreation.

If you're not a gun owner, or if you own a gun for protective purposes only, you might be surprised by just how many of your friends and neighbors are actively involved in the shooting sports. The National Sporting Goods Association estimates there are some 35 million hunters and recreational shooters in the U.S. today. That's more than the number of Americans playing golf, tennis, or skiing.[1]

The enormous popularity of shooting is a reflection of the positive values it instills in participants. For generations, parents have used the shooting sports to teach their children important lessons about discipline and responsibility. Shooting is easy to teach and learn, and builds confidence in young people. And unlike most sports, it puts girls and boys on a level playing field where they compete as equals. Maybe that's why more and more females have taken up shooting in recent years and now constitute the fastest growing segment of the shooting community.

Perhaps what are most important, however, are the benefits of the shooting sports to the community at large, even for those who have never picked up a rifle or shotgun. Hunters, for instance, play a particularly important role in our nation's wildlife management system by helping to control the wildlife population. Overpopulation of a species often leads to cruel deaths by starvation or disease. By harvesting surplus wildlife during the hunting season, hunters help make sure the herd remains healthy and bountiful.

America's hunters also fund the various government agencies that oversee and protect our wildlife habitats. Through federal excise taxes on hunting equipment, hunters contribute nearly $200 million each year to support wildlife management and habitat acquisition and improvement programs. Revenue raised through Federal Duck Stamps, for instance, has been used to purchase more than five million acres of habitat for our refuge system.[2]

But the economic benefits of the shooting sports stretch much further than that. Researchers estimate the hunting and shooting market generates more than $30.9 billion of economic activity every year—that's more than the annual sales of corporate giants like Coca-Cola, Anheuser-Busch, and McDonald's. What's more, 986,000 jobs are supported by the shooting sports—that's more people than are employed by giants like Wal-Mart and Sears.[3]

Of course, none of these facts are necessary to justify the right of Americans to own firearms. The Second Amendment wasn't conceived by the Founding Fathers to protect hunting or recreational shooting. But these numbers and statistics do serve the important purpose of illustrating just how popular the shooting sports are in America and the positive impact they have on our society.

The National Rifle Association believes that preserving this sporting heritage is vitally important. While the NRA's role in the political arena receives plenty of attention from the media, its activities in support of the shooting sports are often overlooked. Nevertheless, the NRA continues to be the biggest booster of the shooting sports in the United States today.

Each year, thousands of shooters compete in NRA-sponsored events, including the National Rifle and Pistol Championships at Camp Perry, Ohio. Thousands more learn how to be responsible gun owners through firearms safety and education programs taught by NRA-certified instructors. And, of course, schoolchildren from coast to coast are taught Eddie Eagle's lifesaving message.

The NRA also works with America's sportsmen to promote safe and ethical hunting practices and sponsors events like the Youth Hunter Education Challenge, which is the most comprehensive youth hunting program in North America, and the Great American Hunters Tour, a world-class event that brings renowned hunters to communities across America to share their insight with local sportsmen.

If you are active in the shooting sports, you already know the rewards and personal satisfaction they offer. The next time you go to the shooting range or take a hunting trip, bring along a friend or relative who hasn't been fortunate enough to try your sport. Getting more people involved in shooting is the best way to ensure that our traditions will be passed on to future generations.

Appendix

Zell Miller's "Picket Line of Freedom"

Zell Miller, the former governor of Georgia and current U.S. senator, is a leading Democrat—and a passionate defender of the Second Amendment. As noted in Chapter Eleven, Senator Miller was the keynote speaker at the NRA's national convention in April of 2002.

Below are Senator Miller's remarks to the convention, in which he speaks about what gun ownership means to him and about the presumed gulf between the NRA and the Democratic Party.

Thank you very much. And thank you, Wayne and Jim, for inviting me to be here tonight and for that introduction. It has been a while since you've had a Democrat as your keynote speaker, and I was honored to accept your invitation.

And as a lifelong country music fan, to be the opening act for Vince Gill is a dream come true. I want his "Go Rest High on That Mountain" played at my funeral.

I'm pleased you mentioned that sharp shooting cousin of mine and I'm proud he could come out here with me. Eric England, would you please stand.

And my Senate colleague, Larry Craig of Idaho, is here also. We are the sponsors of the "Protection of Lawful Commerce in Arms

Act," which addresses the problem of junk lawsuits filed with the intention of driving the firearms industry out of business. These are lawsuits that seek to hold manufacturers and dealers liable for the crimes of others.

Twenty-six states, including my own of Georgia, have already enacted this kind of legislation. The U.S. Congress should follow suit.

I got my first gun—a 20-gauge Stevens—when I was twelve years old, and since that time I've accumulated quite a few others. Like many of you, I've got more guns than I need but not as many as I want.

And, hear this good—I am also a Life Member of the National Rifle Association, with an A+ rating, and I'm proud of it.

Somehow the media and the pundits conveniently overlook that freedom is not partisan. She does not label herself with an "R" or a "D." She welcomes all who would embrace and defend her. She is neither bound by political party, nor heritage, nor station in life, nor evil act of terrorism.

The boundless nature of freedom has never been more evident than it was on September 11. Evil cowards may attack concrete and metal, but they can never destroy the steel of the righteous American heart longing to live free.

President Bush was right when he urged Americans to get back to living, working, and raising our families. To be free, we must live free. I am very proud of our president. Because to defend freedom, we must fight for freedom.

The world must be made safe for democracy, its peace planted upon the foundation of liberty. That is the fight our commander in chief—backed by America's finest in the military—is waging. Peace and liberty are at stake. And I support the president and I know you do, too.

Here at home, in our fight against suicidal terrorists who crash planes into our cities, the most certain line of defense is a skillfully trained, highly dedicated, armed airline pilot. Our pilots want that choice and most Americans support them.

To President Bush and his administration I say this: We trust the pilot with our lives. It's time to trust him with a firearm.

Just a week before this past Christmas, we witnessed the true essence of freedom. On December 18, the oppressed city of Kandahar was liberated by U.S. troops.

Within minutes, the streets of that city were filled with music, men and women dancing with delight, and squealing children playing on homemade, wooden ferris wheels.

Life, liberty, and the pursuit of happiness.

Mr. Heston, you and the other Founding Fathers were pretty doggoned smart when you wrote those words.

Actually, Mr. Heston, you did write, in a letter to your grandson, that "This country is still what it has been from the beginning... an example to the world: Men can live free. In America, democracy works. Not as well as we need it to work sometimes, but we are still, to the rest of the world, the shining door to freedom."

Those words not only fill us with inspiration. They also burden us with duty. America can only serve as that shining door to the world if we remain vigilant in our defense of freedom here at home.

And vigilance is not passive, it is active. Freedom is not a spectator sport for which we cheer from the stands. We—Americans— have to get in the game.

You know, I love baseball. I've played it, coached it, and have been a student and fan of the game all my life. It's been said that if you want to really know America, you have to know baseball.

As an ardent fan of the Second Amendment, I can say this: If you really want to know about defending freedom, you have to know members of the National Rifle Association.

Clearly, your active vigilance was brought to bear in the last election. And make no mistake about it, your efforts in the 2000 elections were joined by tens of thousands of freedom-loving Republicans, independents, and Democrats in states like Arkansas, West Virginia, and Tennessee.

I recall the surprise of national Democratic leaders at losing those states in the presidential election. All their expert pollsters said voters favored gun control.

It reminded me of the time I was running for reelection as governor in 1994. Some of these experts urged me to change my longtime position on guns, telling me that most Georgians favored gun control. Well, I stand with heartfelt conviction over a political wind gauge any day.

But my gut instinct said their polls were wrong. I said, "You're asking the question the wrong way. Ask whether they agree or disagree with this statement: 'Whenever I hear politicians talking about gun control, it makes me wonder if they understand my values or my way of life.'"

You know how many agreed? 73 percent.

What many do not understand is that the gun issue is not just about guns. It's about values. It's about setting priorities. It's about personal freedom; it's about individual responsibility.

And when you get right down to it, that's what elections are about: trust, trust—plain and simple. At the core of a free society is the trust "We the People" place in candidates when we elect them to office to serve our values. And, as Mr. Heston so eloquently stated during the last campaign, "Freedom runs in every race."

Today, our freedom faces a far greater threat than that of any antigun politician. If we don't remain as vigilant as ever, freedom could be lost forever.

A couple of years ago, an Emory University professor named Michael A. Bellesiles wrote the most distorted view ever published about the role of firearms in early America. It was called *Arming America*.

It delighted antigun reviewers by claiming that colonial militias were ineffective, that settlers seldom engaged in hunting, and that colonists had little interest in owning firearms. The *New York Times* gave it a glowing, almost giddy review of several pages, as did the other liberal media.

It would seem that, in Bellesiles's America-in-Wonderland, colonists were a bunch of naive, wishy-washy peaceniks.

Well, tell that to the British Redcoats who tried to cross Concord Bridge!

Tell that to Thomas Jefferson, who said, "No free man shall ever be debarred the use of arms."

Or Samuel Adams, who said, "The Constitution shall never be construed to authorize Congress...to prevent the people of the United States, who are peaceable citizens, from keeping their own arms."

Tell that to James Madison, the Father of the Constitution, who explained that the Constitution preserves "the advantage of being armed which Americans possess over the people of almost every other nation where the governments are afraid to trust the people."

And, Thomas Paine, the writer of *Common Sense*, that pamphlet that inspired the Revolution, who wrote, "Arms discourage and keep the invader and plunderer in awe, and preserve order in the world."

Or finally, Patrick Henry, who warned us to "Guard with jealous attention the public liberty." "Suspect everyone," he said, "who approaches that jewel."

In those words of Patrick Henry, I suspect Professor Bellesiles with the willful intent to kill the Second Amendment. But all his distortion, backed by all the antigun media in the world, cannot murder the Founding Fathers' wisdom that no man be disarmed.

By the way, when other historians later began to really examine the Bellesiles book, which one early reviewer labeled as "the NRA's worst nightmare," these historians found he had actually made up much of his so-called research. Just made it up out of the thin air of antigun bias.

One of the most respected historians at Emory called the research "scholarly incompetence."

And an inquiry is presently under way, as the dean of that university said this week, to address allegations of misconduct in research. An NRA nightmare? I don't think so.

But, my friends, that's the kind of thing we're up against, and it has come down to us—the guardians of the Second Amendment—to ensure the preservation of our heritage.

And we must meet the challenges of our time just as strongly as those who came before us met the challenges in their day.

I urge everyone here in this room to talk to a young person about America's liberty, talk to them about the Second Amendment's meaning of freedom. If we don't do that, I can promise you no one else will.

It is our duty—yours and mine—to pass on to our children and grandchildren the wisdom of the Bill of Rights, that great backbone of freedom.

And if we ever allow one of that backbone's vertebrae to weaken, this country will end up with a permanent curvature of the spine.

I am pleased to see some young faces here in this audience. They are our future. Our children...your children and their children are our future.

The future of our world is on the faces of those children laughing and celebrating liberty in the streets of Kandahar. Our future is in the bright eyes of our grandchildren, eager to ask, "But why?" The future relies upon the unblinking aim of a young shooter and the wonderment of a boy on his first hunt in the woods.

Like the tiny hand of the young girl reaching up to her grandfather's weathered grip, our children reach to us—especially they reach to us during today's troubling times.

If America is to remain the bright doorway of freedom for the world, we must be that shining portal for our children. That is our role and we are duty-bound to serve its just cause.

Another Democrat once put it this way: "In the long history of the world, only a few generations have been granted the role of defending freedom in its hour of maximum danger. I do not shrink from this responsibility—I welcome it."

Those are the words of another NRA Life Member, President John F. Kennedy.

Yes, men can live free. And together, let us welcome our duty in passing that basic tenet on to future generations.

I love America.

The heart of all that is good and right about America is, "One Nation, Under God, Indivisible, With Liberty and Justice for All."

The heart of this great organization pounds with the blood of all those before us who sacrificed their lives in the name of liberty. And our heart must ache with the same yearning of our forefathers: life, liberty, and the pursuit of happiness.

May God bless you all. God bless our great nation. God bless America.

Notes

Chapter One: Piggybacking on Terror

1. Jeffrey Snyder, "A Nation of Cowards," *The Public Interest*, September 22, 1993.
2. Ibid.
3. Jens Ludwig and Philip J. Cook, "Homicide and Suicide Rates Associated with Implementation of the Brady Handgun Violence Prevention Act," *Journal of the American Medical Association*, August 2, 2000.
4. See Urban Institute, "Impact Evaluation of the Public Safety and Recreational Firearms Use Protection Act of 1994," March 13, 1997.
5. John R. Lott, Jr., "The Missing Gun," *New York Post*, January 25, 2002.
6. U.S. Department of Justice, FBI Crime Index.
7. Raymond J. Keating and Thomas N. Edmonds, *U.S. By the Numbers: Figuring What's Left, Right, and Wrong with America State by State* (Sterling, VA: Capital Books, Inc., 2000).
8. Gary Kleck and Marc Gertz, "Armed Resistance to Crime: The Prevalence and Nature of Self-Defense with a Gun," *Journal of Criminal Law and Criminology*, Fall 1995, 150–87.
9. Marvin E. Wolfgang, "A Tribute to a View That I Have Opposed," *Journal of Criminal Law and Criminology*, Fall 1995, 188–92.
10. James D. Wright and Peter H. Rossi, *Armed and Considered Dangerous: A Survey of Felons and Their Firearms* (New York: Aldine de Gruyter, 1991), 155.
11. Sam MacDonald, "An Antigun Firefight," *Insight on the News*, April 22, 2002.
12. Ibid.

13. Ibid.
14. James Norrell, "Gun Control's Great Petri Dish," *American Rifleman*, March 2002.
15. Matt Bai, "The 'Angel' in a Shoot-out," *Newsweek*, October 9, 2000.
16. James L. Pate, "Americans for Gun Safety May Be the Name..." *American Rifleman*, July 2001.
17. Wayne LaPierre, "Standing Guard," *American Rifleman*, July 2001.
18. Pate, "Americans for Gun Safety May Be the Name...."
19. Ibid.

Chapter Two: Your Handbook on Gun Issues

1. Rick Montgomery, "Rampage Report Only Part of Story, Gun Lobby Says," *Kansas City Star*, March 6, 2002.
2. Keating and Edmonds, *U.S. By the Numbers*.
3. AGS statement, December 14, 2001.
4. James Baker, "Anti-gun Lobby Misfires: Targeting Gun Shows Won't Stop Terrorism," *Washington Times*, December 20, 2001.
5. H. Sterling Burnett, "The Gun Show 'Loophole,'" *American Rifleman*, May 2001.
6. Interview, Wayne LaPierre, April 8, 2002.
7. Burnett, "The Gun Show 'Loophole.'"
8. Ibid.
9. Ibid.
10. Ibid.
11. "Canada: Where Gun Registration Equals Confiscation," *American Rifleman*, March 2001.
12. Ibid.
13. Ibid.
14. Ibid.
15. Ibid.
16. Norrell, "Gun Control's Great Petri Dish."
17. Burnett, "The Gun Show 'Loophole.'"
18. Report for Congress: Firearms Regulations in Various Foreign Countries, May 1998.
19. Daniel D. Polsby, "The False Promise of Gun Control," *Atlantic Monthly*, March 1994.

20. Caroline E. Mayer, "Safety Standards Sought After Gun Locks Fail Test," *Washington Post*, February 7, 2001.
21. "Master Lock Recalling 750,000 Gun Locks," NBC's *Today*, July 25, 2000.
22. Mayer, "Safety Standards Sought After Gun Locks Fail Test."
23. Kenneth Smith, "No Self-Defense Allowed?" *Washington Times*, May 11, 2000; NRA video.
24. NRA Fact Sheet, "Defending CDC's National Center for Injury Prevention and Control," July 29, 1999.
25. Ibid.
26. Ibid.
27. Ibid.
28. NRA video.
29. Interview, Wayne LaPierre; NRA Fact Sheet, July 29, 1999.
30. NRA Fact Sheet, July 29, 1999.
31. Phillip McGuire, Testimony Before the House Subcommittee on Crime, May 15, 1986.
32. Ibid.
33. Speech by Sandra S. Froman, California Rifle and Pistol Association, posted July 23, 2001.
34. Josh Sugarmann, "Assault Weapons and Accessories in America," The Educational Fund to End Handgun Violence and the New Right Watch, September 1988.
35. NRA Fact Sheet, "Semi-automatic Firearms," July 29, 2000.
36. Ibid.
37. Ibid.
38. Ibid.
39. Ibid.
40. Speech by Froman.
41. "Hyping the Crime Bill," *Washington Post*, September 15, 1994.
42. Department of the Treasury, BATF, "A Study Concerning the Threat to Law Enforcement Officers from the Criminal Use of Firearms and Ammunition," 1998.
43. Bureau of Justice Statistics, "Criminal Victimization 1997, Changes 1996–1997, with Trends 1993–1997," December 1998.
44. Wright and Rossi, *Armed and Considered Dangerous*.
45. Gary Kleck, *Targeting Guns: Firearms and Their Control* (New York: Aldine de Gruyter, 1997); Gary Kleck, *Point*

Blank: Guns and Violence in America (New York: Aldine de Gruyter, 1991).

46. James D. Wright, et al., *Under the Gun: Weapons, Crime, and Violence in America* (New York: Aldine Publishing Co., 1983); James D. Wright and Peter H. Rossi, *Armed and Considered Dangerous: A Survey of Felons and Their Firearms* (New York: Aldine de Gruyter, 1986).

47. *Dred Scott* v. *Sanford*, 19 How. 393, (1857), 98.

48. Robert Sherrill, *The Saturday Night Special: and Other Guns with Which Americans Won the West, Protected Bootleg Franchises, Slew Wildlife, Robbed Countless Banks, Shot Husbands Purposely and by Mistake, and Killed Presidents—Together with the Debate Over Continuing Same* (New York: Charterhouse, 1973).

49. Tony Mauro, "2nd Amendment: A Right to Own Arms?" *USA Today*, November 20, 1991.

50. NRA Fact Sheet, July 29, 1999.

51. Interview, Wayne LaPierre.

52. Ibid.

53. Edward Walsh, "ATF Firearms Prosecution Referrals Drop," *Washington Post*, August 29, 1999.

54. "ATF Criminal Referrals in Relation to District Population, 1998," available at http://trac.syr.edu/tracatf/findings/98/criminal/refR98.html.

55. Jeff Sessions, "Guns: What Works, What Doesn't," *Washington Times*, May 15, 2000.

56. "Justice Department Provides $70M in Funds to Promote Gun Violence Prosecution," U.S. Newswire, January 23, 2002.

Chapter Three: Citizen Rights

1. Ed Housewright, "Victims Praised as Caring, Involved Relatives," *Dallas Morning News*, October 18, 1991; David McLemore and Doug J. Swanson, " 'None of Us Were Prepared': Killeen Loses Faith in Safety of Small Town," *Dallas Morning News*, October 20, 1991.

2. Timothy Wheeler, "Life and Death in the City," *San Diego Union-Tribune*, May 31, 2000.

3. Interview, Wayne LaPierre.

4. Mitch Stacy, "Former '60s Radical Rap Brown Sentenced to Life in Prison," Associated Press, March 14, 2002.
5. Wayne LaPierre, NBC's *Meet the Press*, March 19, 2000.
6. ABC News, March 15, 2000.
7. John R. Lott, Jr., *More Guns, Less Crime: Understanding Crime and Gun-Control Laws* (Chicago: University of Chicago Press, 1998), 13.
8. Ibid., 13.
9. NRA quote of *Warren* v. *District of Columbia*, 444 A.2nd 1, (1981).
10. Lott, *More Guns, Less Crime*, 36.
11. Tom Diaz, "Fresh Air," National Public Radio, January 20, 1999.
12. Tom Jackson, "Keeping the Battle Alive," *Tampa Tribune*, October 21, 1993.
13. Mauro, "2nd Amendment: A Right to Own Arms?"
14. NRA Fact Sheet, "Brady Campaign (Handgun Control, Inc.) 2001 'Report Card' Again Gives Higher 'Grades' to States with Higher Violent Crime Rates," January 24, 2002.
15. Jim Keary, "Children 'Taunted' in Zoo Shootings," *Washington Times*, May 13, 2000.
16. Ibid.
17. NRA Fact Sheet, May 28, 1999.
18. Ibid.
19. Carlos Sanchez, "Columnist Rowan Shoots Back Yard Intruder," *Washington Post*, June 15, 1988.
20. Lieutenant Dennis Tueller of the Salt Lake City Police Department, Testimony Before the House Judiciary Committee, Crime Review of Gun Laws, April 5, 1995. Statistic based on a June 1993 survey by the Southern States Police Benevolent Association.
21. Tueller, Testimony Before the House Judiciary Committee. Statistics based on a 1994 survey by the Police Marksman Association and a survey from the July–August 1991 issue of *Law Enforcement Technology*.
22. NBC's *Meet the Press*, March 19, 2000.
23. John Russi, Testimony Before the Michigan House of Representatives Judiciary Committee, November 5, 1995.
24. Rebecca John, "Fears of Gun-Carry Law Are Unfounded," *Denver Post*, April 15, 1995.

25. John R. Lott, Jr., "The Bush Record on Guns," *Washington Times*, October 10, 2000.
26. John R. Lott, Jr., and David B. Mustard, "Crime, Deterrence, and Right-to-Carry Concealed Handguns," *Journal of Legal Studies*, Vol. 26, January 1997.
27. Kleck, *Targeting Guns*, 178.
28. "Wounded Wrestler Hailed as Hero," *Houston Chronicle*, May 24, 1998.
29. Snyder, "A Nation of Cowards."
30. Lott, *More Guns, Less Crime*, 20.

Chapter Four: (Real) Homeland Defense

1. Al Baker, "A Nation Challenged: Personal Security: Steep Rise in Gun Sales Reflects Post-Attack Fears," *New York Times*, December 16, 2001.
2. Jacqueline L. Salmon, "Sept. 11 Donations, Economy Leave Many Nonprofits Strapped," *Washington Post*, October 9, 2001.
3. Paul Harvey read this widely circulated essay on his radio show in October 2001. The original author is unknown.
4. Edwin Meese III and Kim Holmes, "Balancing Security and Liberty," *Washington Times*, October 16, 2001.
5. Etgar Lefkovits, "Gun Demand Up 75 Percent," *Jerusalem Post*, March 7, 2002.
6. Tim Johnson, "Israelis Go 'On Alert,' Foil Suicide Bombings," *Miami Herald*, February 23, 2002.
7. Joseph A. Reaves, "WWII Air Ace Runs Afoul of Security," *Arizona Republic*, February 16, 2000.
8. Sally B. Donnelly, "Airline Security: Stuck on the Runway?" www.time.com, April 21, 2002.
9. John R. Lott, Jr., "Arming Pilots Is the Best Way to Get Air Security," LATimes.com, March 11, 2002.
10. Ann Coulter, "Would Mohammed Atta Object to Armed Pilots?" Townhall.com, May 30, 2002.
11. Ibid.
12. Wayne LaPierre, "Standing Guard," *American Rifleman*, December 2001.

13. Lott, "Arming Pilots Is the Best Way to Get Air Security."
14. "Teenager Shot Twice in Cockpit After Flight from Texas," *Chicago Sun-Times*, October 25, 2001.
15. John J. Miller and Ramesh Ponnuru, "Alien Invasion," National Review Online, October 24, 2001.

Chapter Five: Gun Safety

1. Tracey A. Reeves, "Md. House Passes Gun Education," *Washington Post*, April 6, 2001.
2. Daniel Le Duc and Tracey A. Reeves, "Md. Gun Safety Classes Vetoed," *Washington Post*, May 18, 2001.
3. NRA Fact Sheet, ".50-caliber Rifles—Latest Bugaboo from Anti-gun Fringe," August 28, 2001.
4. NRA-ILA, "Once Upon a Time...Fables, Myths, and Other Tall Tales about Gun Laws, Crime, and Constitutional Rights," www.nraila.org.
5. NRA Fact Sheet, "Smart Guns," January 27, 2000.

Chapter Six: Second Amendment Follies

1. Anne Gearan, "Justice Department Reverses Stance on Whether Constitution Includes Individual Right to Bear Arms," Associated Press, May 8, 2002.
2. Stephen P. Halbrook, *That Every Man Be Armed: The Evolution of a Constitutional Right* (Albuquerque: University of New Mexico Press, 1984), 17.
3. Tench Coxe, *Pennsylvania Gazette*, February 20, 1788.
4. *The Federalist*, Number 29.
5. Senator Larry Craig, statement on the Senate floor, June 6, 2000.
6. Neely Tucker and Arthur Santana, "D.C. Handgun Ban Challenged in Court," *Washington Post*, May 30, 2002.
7. Michael Barnes, press statement, April 18, 2001.
8. Michael Korda, "Loaded Words," *American Rifleman*, November 2001.
9. Melissa Seckora, "Disarming America, Part II," National Review Online, November 26, 2001.

10. Clayton Cramer, *American Rifleman*, January 2001.
11. Stephen P. Halbrook, *American Rifleman*, January 2001.
12. David Skinner, "The Cowards of Academe," *Weekly Standard*, June 10, 2002.
13. Martin Miller, "Attack on the Clunes," *Los Angeles Times*, May 21, 2002.
14. The rifle is now on display in the NRA's National Firearms Museum.
15. Mark A. Keefe IV, *American Rifleman*, April 2002.

Chapter Seven: The Gun-Control Hive

1. Gary Aldrich, "Ohio Rifles Stand as Symbols," Townhall.com, April 30, 2002.
2. Lott, *More Guns, Less Crime*, 122–23.
3. Peter H. Stone, "Plenty of Firepower," *National Journal*, July 22, 2000.
4. Ibid.
5. Ibid.
6. www.vpc.org/fact_sht/eddiekey.htm.
7. Stone, "Plenty of Firepower."
8. www.doctorsagainsthandguninjury.org/position.html.
9. "Is There a Gun in the House?" CBS's *60 Minutes*, May 12, 2002.
10. Martha T. Moore, "Tycoon Puts His Money Where His Beliefs Are," *USA Today*, August 25, 1997; David B. Ottaway, "Legal Assault on Firms Is Armed by Foundations," *Washington Post*, May 19, 1999.
11. Mark Johnson, "Political Gravity Tugs Grants to Left," *Richmond Times-Dispatch*, May 3, 1998.

Chapter Eight: The Litigation Machine

1. Adam Cohen, "Are Lawyers Running America?" *Time*, July 17, 2000.
2. Mike France, "The Litigation Machine," *Business Week*, January 29, 2001.
3. "Insuring Against Terrorism," *New York Times*, June 8, 2002; John Ashworth and James Moore, "U.S. Legal Fight May Mean

No End to the Nightmare on Lime Street," *Times* (London), July 16, 2001.

4. France, "The Litigation Machine."
5. Cohen, "Are Lawyers Running America?"
6. Max Schulz, "Smoking Guns," *Reason*, July 1998.
7. John R. Lott, Jr., "Gun Shy," *National Review*, December 21, 1998.
8. Frank J. Murray, "Gun Makers Tough Targets for Cities," *Washington Times*, March 10, 1999.
9. Fox Butterfield, "Suit Against Gun Makers Gains Ground in Illinois," *New York Times*, January 3, 2002.
10. Lott, "Gun Shy."
11. NRA Fact Sheet, " 'Unsafe Handgun Act': Target for Trial Attorneys," May 22, 2001.
12. David E. Rosenbaum, "Echoes of Tobacco Battle in Gun Suits," *New York Times*, March 21, 1999.
13. "Texas Forbids Cities to Sue Gun Firms," *Washington Post*, June 20, 1999.
14. Stephen Dinan, "Court Spurns Lawsuit on Guns as 'Nuisance,' " *Washington Times*, January 16, 2002.
15. Carolyn Barta, "Cities Look to Courts in Fight Against Gun-Related Crimes," *Dallas Morning News*, June 6, 1999.
16. "A Defeat for Gun Control," *Washington Times*, October 11, 2001.
17. NRA Fact Sheet, "Firearms Preemption Laws," July 29, 1999.

Chapter Nine: Hollywood and Guns

1. Larry Elder, "The 'SAP' Awards," FrontPageMagazine.com, April 5, 2002.
2. Ibid.
3. Ibid.
4. M. Christine Klein, "Patsy Get Your Gun: Rosie Needs It," National Review Online, May 25, 2000.
5. Korda, "Loaded Words."
6. Representative J. C. Watts, keynote address to the National Rifle Association Annual Convention, Charlotte, N.C., May 20, 2000.
7. Charlton Heston, address to Harvard Law School, February 16, 1999.

8. FTC press release, "FTC Releases Report on the Marketing of Violent Entertainment to Children," September 11, 2000.
9. Daniel B. Borenstein, M.D., Testimony Before the Senate Committee on Commerce, Science, and Transportation, September 13, 2000.
10. Joint Statement on the Impact of Entertainment Violence on Children, Congressional Public Health Summit, July 26, 2000.
11. Ibid.
12. Shankar Vedantam, "Study Ties Television Viewing to Aggression," *Washington Post*, March 29, 2002.
13. Ibid.

Chapter Ten: Little Acorns and Bad Treaties

1. "Gun Control Movement Goes International," PR Newswire, July 17, 2001.
2. Report for Congress: "Firearms Regulations in Various Foreign Countries," Library of Congress, May 1998.
3. Cathy Young, "The Bias Against Handguns," *Boston Globe*, March 18, 2002.
4. Philip Bourjaily, "Champions of Civil Markmanship," *American Rifleman*, November 29, 2001.
5. NRA Fact Sheet, "Gun Laws, Culture, Justice, and Crime in Foreign Countries," April 10, 2001.
6. Ibid.
7. Ibid.
8. Ibid.
9. Ibid.
10. NRA Fact Sheet, "The United Nations and Gun Control," July 29, 1999.
11. Betsy Pisik, "U.S. Negotiators Wary of Pact to Curb Small-arms Sales," *Washington Times*, April 12, 2001.
12. Ibid.
13. Barbara Crossette, "Effort by U.N. to Cut Traffic in Arms Meets a U.S. Rebuff," *New York Times*, July 10, 2001.
14. Betsy Pisik, "U.S. Wins on Guns Despite Foreign Anger," *Washington Times*, July 22, 2001.

15. "An American Retreat on Small Arms," *New York Times*, July 11, 2001.
16. Crossette, "Effort by U.N. to Cut Traffic in Arms Meets a U.S. Rebuff."

Chapter Eleven: Gun Control and "Silver Bullets"

1. Jeffrey H. Birnbaum, "Fat and Happy in D.C.," *Fortune*, May 28, 2001.
2. Snyder, "A Nation of Cowards."
3. "Shootout: Gun-Control Groups Getting Stronger," *Columbus Dispatch*, August 1, 2000.
4. Eunice Moscoso, "Convention an Island of Calm in a Gun-Control Storm," Cox News Service, August 3, 2000.
5. Otis Bilodeau, "Gun Control Advocates Gain a Little Ground," *Legal Times*, November 13, 2000.
6. Stephen Dinan, "Caller Ties Son's Killing to Allen's Policy," *Washington Times*, November 4, 2000.
7. Lott, *More Guns, Less Crime*, 38.
8. Congressman Richard Gephardt, CNN's *Inside Politics*, August 7, 2001.
9. Matt Bai, "Red Zone vs. Blue Zone," *Newsweek*, January 22, 2001.
10. Joe Julavits, "Notebook," *Florida Times-Union*, February 4, 2001.
11. Charlie Cook, November 9, 2000, NRA Web site quote.
12. NRA-ILA Fax Alert, Vol. 7, No. 5, December 21, 2000.
13. Howard Fineman, " 'King Karl' Gets Ready," *Newsweek*, June 3, 2002.
14. Allison Stevens, "Dems Abandon Gun Issue in 2002 Races," *The Hill*, May 22, 2002.
15. Mark Obmascik, "Guns Still in Political Cross Hairs," *Denver Post*, May 12, 2002.
16. Lynn Bartels, "Virginia Group Outspends NRA in Battle Over Amendment 22," *Denver Rocky Mountain News*, October 24, 2000.
17. Bilodeau, "Gun Control Advocates Gain a Little Ground."
18. Bartels, "Virginia Group Outspends NRA in Battle Over Amendment 22."
19. Bilodeau, "Gun Control Advocates Gain a Little Ground."

20. Mike Soraghan, "Terror Ads Tag Along with Allard: Stance Cited on Defense, Gun Control," *Denver Post*, April 30, 2002.
21. NRA Fact Sheet, "Firearms Facts 2002," Lawrence Research— National survey of registered voters, 1998.

Conclusion

1. Snyder, "A Nation of Cowards."

Postscript

1. National Sporting Goods Association, "Sports Participation in 2001" survey, www.nsga.org.
2. U.S. Fish and Wildlife Service, www.fws.gov.
3. National Shooting Sports Foundation, www.nssf.org.

Acknowledgments

The authors wish to acknowledge the following individuals for their contributions to this book: Patrick O'Malley, for his editorial guidance; Mark Davis, for his creative expertise; Michael Smith, for providing research and editorial assistance; and Tom Edmonds, our political consultant turned book agent who helped put this project together. We'd also like to thank the staff members of the National Rifle Association, too numerous to name, who have supported and assisted in the effort to protect the Second Amendment over the years.

Index

AARP, 150, 161
Adams, Samuel, 187
Aeschylus, 144
Afghanistan, 2, 10, 88, 142, 173
AFL-CIO, 128, 167
Africa, 84
African-Americans, 50–51
AGS. *See* Americans for Gun Safety
Air Egypt, 89
Airline Pilots' Security Alliance, 90
airport security, 58, 87–89
Alabama, 56, 60–61
Al-Amin, Jamil Abdullah, 61–62
Alaska, 102
Aldrich, Gary, 121–22
Allard, Wayne, 168–69
Allen, George F., 165
Alameda County, Calif., 135
AMA. *See* American Medical Association
America: crime in, 5, 18, 59–80, 151–52; Founders and, 2, 5, 19, 57; gun ownership in, ix, 44; gun safety in, 40–41; guns in early, 113–18; right-to-carry laws in, 74–75; self-defense in, 119; spirit of, 1–2, 173–75; terrorism and, 5
American Association of School Administrators, 128
American Bar Association, 124, 128
American Civil Liberties Union, 13, 128
American Federation of Teachers, 128
Americans for Democratic Action, 128
American Medical Association (AMA), 125–26

American Psychiatric Association, 146
American Revolution, 113
American Rifleman, 116, 117
Americans for Gun Safety (AGS), 169; agenda of, 126; campaign finance reform and, 23; funding for, 14–15, 16; gun safety education and, 16; gun shows and, 24–26; image of, 16; intentions of, 15; staffing of, 15–16; tactics of, 16; terrorism and gun control and, 12–13; women and, 16
Amnesty International, 150, 155
Amory, Cleveland, 101
Anderson, Jack, 41–42
Angelos, Peter, 132
Anheuser-Busch, 180
Animal Liberation Front, 101
Animal Rights Reporter, 101
Anniston, Ala., 60–61
antigun groups: agenda of, 120–28; constitutionality of gun ownership and, 12–13; funding for, 14–15, 22, 126–28
antique guns, 48–49
Appalachian School of Law, 7–8
Aristotle, 107
Arizona, 87
Arkansas, 165
Arming America: The Origins of a National Gun Culture (Bellesiles), 114, 186
"Army and Navy" law of 1879, 51
Aryan Nation, 63
Ashcroft, John, 56, 106, 111
"assault weapons": "Crime Bill" of 1994 and, 46–47; deceit about, 18, 43–47;

"assault weapons" *(continued)*
definition of, 43–44; federal ban on, 6–7; semi-automatic firearms and, 7, 21–22
Atlanta, Ga., 134
Atta, Mohammed, 89
Audubon, 100
Augustine, Saint, 107
Australia: gun control and, 34, 154; registration and confiscation and, 57; self-defense and, 149

background checks: Brady Act and, 6; gun control and, 30, 55; gun shows and, 24, 26, 27–28; mental records and, 29; NRA and, 30; terrorism and, 81
Baker, James Jay, ix, 168
Baldwin, Alec, 140
ballistic fingerprinting, 47–48
Baltimore, Md., 63
Baltimore Fraternal Order of Police, 72
Barnes, Michael, 114, 124
Barondess, Jeremiah, 121, 125
Barr, Bob, 149, 158
Bartlet, Josiah, 139–40, 165
Bates, Harris, 66
BATF. *See* Bureau of Alcohol, Tobacco, and Firearms
Beamer, Todd, 1
Begala, Paul, 163, 164
Bellesiles, Michael A., 186, 187; guns in early America and, 114–18
Belton, Tex., 60
Ben & Jerry's, 128
Benelli Field Auto Shotgun, 44
Beretta, 98
Berg, Alan, 63
Besen, Ted, 8
big media. *See* media
Bill of Rights, 52, 107
bin Laden, Osama, 83, 84
Birdsong, Ricky, 62
Blackstone, Sir William, 108
Bloomington, Ind., 62
Boer War, 152
Bolton, John R., 158, 159
Bonnell, William, 91
border control, 91–92
Borenstein, Daniel B., 146
Boston, Mass., 135
Boumelhem, Ali, 12, 25
Bourjaily, Philip, 152

Boxer, Barbara, 35
Brady Act, 6–7
Brady Center to Prevent Gun Violence, 81; agenda of, 123–24; self-defense and, 65; terrorism and gun control and, 10
Brady, Jim and Sarah, 52, 123
Brazil, 150
Bridgeport, Conn., 134
Bridges, Tracy, 7–8
Britain. *See* Great Britain
Brown, H. Rap, 61
Bureau of Alcohol, Tobacco, and Firearms (BATF): antique guns and, 49; "assault weapons" and, 47; conversion and, 45; "cop-killer" bullets hoax and, 35; gun crime and, 55; gun shows and, 26; "Saturday night specials" and, 49; self-defense and, 65
Burnett, Deena, 1
Burnett, H. Sterling, 31
Burnett, Tom, 1, 173
Bush, George W., 1; crime and morality and, 3; economic legislation of, 23; Election 2000 and, 164; gun control and, 56, 136; law-enforcement community and, 77; Texas right-to-carry laws and, 76
Bushman, Brad, 147
Business Week, 132
Butterfield, Fox, 135
Buzzword Factory, 47; "child-safety locks" and, 38; "cop-killer" bullets hoax and, 35; plastic gun sham and, 41, 42; terms of debate and, 22
Byrd, James, 163

Cairo, Egypt, 156
California, 46; crime in, 35; gun control and, 71, 74; gun registration in, 31; registration and confiscation and, 34, 43; waiting periods in, 35
Cambodia, 129, 150
campaign finance reform, 13–15, 23, 57, 133
Canada, 174; crime in, 32–33; gun control and, 153–54; gun control and crime and, 151; gun registration in, 31; individual rights in, 31; Parliament in, 32; registration and confiscation and, 31–33, 57; self-defense and, 149; suicide in, 152
Canadian Firearms Act, 32, 154

Canadian Institute for Legislative Action, 32
Cape Fear, 144
Carville, James, 167–68
Castro, Fidel, 129, 149
CATO Institute, 113
CBS, 43
Center for Science in the Public Interest, 129
Centers for Disease Control and Prevention, 40, 125
Center to Prevent Handgun Violence, 124, 134
Centre for Defence Studies, 33
Charles II (king of England), 108
Charlotte Observer, 8
Chicago, Ill., 70–71, 134
Chicago Housing Authority, 96
Chicago Transit Authority, 95–96
children: gun accidents and, 96–97; gun safety and, 18, 40, 94–98
Children's Defense Fund, 151
"child-safety locks." *See* gun safety
China, 129, 159
Churchill, Winston, 120
Cicero, 107
citizen choice, gun safety and, 18, 37–41
Civil Aviation Security, 42
civil rights, guns and, 50–52
Civil War, 51
Cleveland, Ohio, 165
Clinton, Bill, 15; background checks and, 29, 30; "Crime Bill" of 1994 and, 46; gun "buybacks" and, 37; gun control and, 51, 54–55, 67; gun shows and, 84; NRA and, 167; semi-automatic firearms and, 44; terrorism and, 83–84
Clinton, Hillary, 141
Clune, Gordon, 118–19
CNBC, 142
Coca-Cola, 180
Colorado, 16, 169
Columbine school massacre, 143, 145
Common Cause, 128
Common Sense (Paine), 187
concealed weapons, 5
Concord, Mass., 117, 119
confiscation: government and, 31; registration and, 31–34, 43, 70–71
Connecticut, 134
Constitution, 107; Equal Protection clause of, 52; meaning of, 19; militias

and, 57; right to keep and bear arms and, 3; as social contract, 110–11
Consumer Federation of America, 124–25
conversion myth, 45–46
Conyers, John, 11
Cook, Charlie, 166–67
"cooling off" periods. *See* waiting periods
Cooper, James Fenimore, 114, 164
"cop-killer" bullets hoax, 18, 35–36
Coronado, Rod, 101
corporations, antigun group funding and, 14, 22, 128
Coulter, Ann, 90
Cowan, Jonathan, 24; AGS and, 15
Cox, Chris W., 10, 22, 89, 98, 126
Coxe, Tench, 109
Craig, Larry, 59, 79, 110–11, 183
Cramer, Clayton, 115, 116
crime: in America, 18, 59–80; antique guns and, 48–49; "assault weapons" and, 45; freedom and, 3; gun "buybacks" and, 37; gun control and, 4–10, 18, 33–34, 55, 69–80, 97, 151; gun locks and, 38, 39–40; morality and, 3–5; petty, 5; Second Amendment and, 18, 59–60; sentencing and, 5; social contract and, 3; terrorism and, 18; waiting periods and, 35
"Crime Bill" of 1994, 46
Cuba, 129, 149, 159
Cuomo, Andrew, 15–16, 127
Cuomo, Mario, 163–64

Dallas, Tex., 136
Dallas Police Association, 77
Davis, Gray, 135
Declaration of Rights, 108
Dees-Thomases, Donna, 141
democracies in peril, 151–56
Democratic Party: gun control and, 165–71; NRA and, 162–63, 166, 183
Denver, Colo., 63
Detroit, Mich., 135, 165
Dingell, John, 162
discrimination, gun ownership and, 49–52
Disney Corporation, 13, 128
Doctors Against Handgun Injury, 125–26
Doctors for Responsible Gun Ownership, 125

Dole, Bob, 166
Doyle, Arthur Conan, 152
Dred Scott v. *Sanford*, 50–51
Ducks Unlimited, 102
Dunkirk (World War II), 119

Earth First!, 101
Eddie Eagle GunSafe program, 41,
    95–96, 98, 124, 181
Edelman, Marion Wright, 173
education. *See* gun safety
Egypt, 159
Eisner, Michael, 128
Elder, Larry, 141–42
Election 2000, 164–67
Emory University, 114
England. *See* Great Britain
English, Aldranon, 62
Enough, 107
Equal Protection clause, 52
Erin Brockovich, 131
European Union, 174
Evanston, Ill., 71

FAA. *See* Federal Aviation Administra-
    tion
Family Research Library, 116
Fatal Attraction, 144
FBI. *See* Federal Bureau of Investiga-
    tion
Federal Aviation Administration (FAA),
    42, 89
Federal Bureau of Investigation (FBI):
    Boumelhem and, 25; gun control
    and crime and, 6; gun shows and,
    26–27; terrorism and, 85
Federal Duck Stamps, 180
Federal Trade Commission (FTC), 146
Feinstein, Dianne, 49; "assault rifle"
    deceit and, 43
Field & Stream, 100
Finland, 69, 152
firearms. *See* guns
Firearms Act of 1920, 33
Firearms Control Regulations Act
    (1976), 68
Firearms Owners' Protection Act
    (1986), 52
First Amendment, 14, 57, 58, 110
Florida: crime in, 76; gun shows in, 24;
    right-to-carry laws in, 64–65, 75–76
Florida Police Chiefs Association, 75
Florida Sheriffs Association, 75
foreign policy, terrorism and, 83–84

Foreman, Dave, 101
Fortune magazine, 161
Foss, Joe, 88, 89
foundations, antigun group funding
    and, 127–28
Founders: America and, 2; Second
    Amendment and, 2, 57–58, 106,
    108–9, 111; self-defense and, 108;
    vision for America of, 2, 5, 19, 57
Fox, Michael W., 100
Fox News, 142
France, 152
Franklin, Benjamin, 109
Fraternal Order of Police, 77
freedom: crime and, 3; defense of, 2;
    gun control and, 161, 184–89;
    media and, 184; personal, ix; right
    to keep and bear arms and, 57; Sec-
    ond Amendment and, 2, 129; ter-
    rorism and, 84–86
Friday the 13th, 145
Froman, Sandra, 43
FTC. *See* Federal Trade Commission
Fund for Animals, 101
Furrow, Buford, 46

Game Act, 108
Garwood, William L., 111–12
General Accounting Office, 30
General Electric, 13
George Gund Foundation, 127
George III (king of England), 119
George Mason University, 37
Georgia, 71, 136
Gephardt, Richard, 166
Germany, 120, 129, 151, 155
Gertz, Mark, 9
Gill, Vince, 183
Gladiator, 144
Glendening, Parris, 39–40, 94–95
Glick, Susan, 122–23
Glorious Revolution of 1688, 108
Gore, Al, 15; Election 2000 and, 164,
    165; gun control and, 67; gun locks
    and, 66
Granada Hills, Calif., 46
Gratia, Al, 59–60, 173
Gratia, Ursula "Suzy" Kunath, 59–60
Gratia-Hupp, Suzanna, 59–60, 76
Gravano, Salvatore "Sammy the Bull,"
    39
Gray Panthers, 128
Great Britain: common law of, 33;
    crime in, 152; gun control and,

33–34, 74, 152–53; individual rights in, 31; registration and confiscation and, 57; Second Amendment and, 119–20; self-defense and, 149
Great Society, 68
Green, Mark, 96
Green, Tom, 145
Greenberg, Stan, 167–68
Gross, Mikael, 7–8
Grundy, Va., 7–8
gun "buybacks," 37
gun control: background checks and, 29–30, 55; crime and, 4–10, 18, 33–34, 55, 69–80, 97, 151; Democratic Party and, 165–71; Election 2000 and, 164–67; freedom and, 161, 184–89; gun safety and, 23; Hollywood and, 22, 139–48; international, 18, 149–59; litigation and, 131–37; lobby for, 9, 17, 22, 24, 30, 36, 43; media and, 7, 21–24; police and, 72–74; power and, 130; purpose of, 17; registration and, 11; self-defense and, 33, 59–80; "soundbite issues" and, 23–24; terrorism and, 1–19, 10–13, 81–82, 86–87; Utopia and, 128–29; waiting periods and, 13. See also gun locks; gun ownership; guns; gun safety; gun shows
Gun Control Act of 1968, 51, 52, 68
gun locks: crime and, 38; criminals and, 39–40; mandatory issuance of, 17; problem with, 39–40; safety and, 37–41. See also gun control; gun ownership; guns; gun safety; gun shows
gun ownership: in America, ix, 44; constitutionality of, 12–13; discrimination and, 49–52; opposition to, 19; responsibility and, ix, 57, 96; women and, 5, 16, 79–80. See also gun control; gun locks; guns; gun safety; gun shows
guns: accidents with, 40–41, 96–97; alteration of, 52–53; antique, 48–49; availability of, 62–63, 66–70; "buybacks" of, 18, 36–37; civil rights and, 50–52; collecting of, 48–49; conversion myth and, 45–46; in early America, 113–18; as health issue, 125–26; Hollywood and, 175; manufacturers of, 133–36; in movies, 143–47; myths about, ix, 67; for personal safety, 13; plastic,

18, 41–43; registration and confiscation of, 31–34; self-defense and, 7–10; smart, 97–98. See also gun control; gun locks; gun ownership; gun safety; gun shows
gun safety: in America, 40–41; children and, 18, 40; citizen choice and, 18, 37–41; education and, 16, 93–99; gun control and, 23; in homes, 38; legislation for, 17; NRA and, 14; sport shooting and, 98–99. See also gun control; gun locks; gun ownership; guns; gun shows
gun shows: AGS and, 16, 24–26; background checks and, 24, 26, 27–28; Middle East and, 26; NICS and, 27, 30–31; terrorism and, 14, 18, 24–31, 84–85. See also gun control; gun locks; gun ownership; guns; gun safety

Halbrook, Stephen P., 117
Hall, Rush Baynard, 116
Halloween, 145
Hamas, 12
Hamilton, Alexander, 109
Hamlet (Shakespeare), 144
Hammer, Marion P., 75–76
Handgun Control, Inc., 14. See also Brady Center to Prevent Gun Violence
handguns. See "Saturday night specials"; guns
Harper's, 100
Harris, Eric, 143–44, 145
Hart, Peter, 164
Harvey, Paul, 83–84
Heinlein, Robert, 80
Hennard, George, 60
Henry, Patrick, 57, 173, 187
Henry II (king of England), 108
Hession, John, 120
Heston, Charlton, 2, 121, 142, 143
Hezbollah, 12
Hickey, Don, 118
Hitler, Adolf, 129
Hollywood, gun control and, 22, 139–48, 175
Honduras, 150
Horace, 107
Howard, Patricia Kunz, 95
HSUS. See Humane Society of the United States
Hughes-McCollum bill, 43

Humane Society of the United States
(HSUS), 100
hunting: NRA and, 102–3; Second
Amendment and, 59
Hyde, Henry, 140

IBM, 14
Ice-T, 144
Illinois, 134–35; gun control and, 72
Indiana, 62
Inhumane Society, 100
Institute for Legislative Action, 11
Iran, 149
Iraq, 149, 158
Ireland, 25
Israel, 151, 152, 158
Israelis, 86–87

Jamail, Joe, 132
Japan, 152, 155–56, 156–59, 174
Jefferson, Thomas, 107, 109, 187; con-
cealed weapons and, 50; guns in
early America and, 117; terrorism
and, 83
Joe Camel, 96
Johnson, Lyndon, 68
Johnson, Samuel, 168
Jones, Antoine Bernard, 66, 67
Jones, James Antonio, 66
Journal of Legal Studies, 122
Joyce Foundation, 127
Justice Department: "cop-killer" bullets
hoax and, 36; gun "buybacks" of, 36;
gun control and, 56; NICS and, 11;
"Saturday night specials" and, 50

Kandahar, Afghanistan, 185, 188
Kansas, 6
Kansas City, Mo., 165
Kennedy, John F., 188
Kennedy, Robert, 51
Kennedy, Ted, 11, 56, 84
Kennesaw, Ga., 71
Kentucky, 65
Kenya, 150
Khobar Towers, 84
Killeen (Tex.) shooting, 59–60
Kinchen, Ricky, 62
King, Martin Luther, Jr., 51
King's College, 33
Kinkel, Kipland "Kip," 78–79
Kipling, Rudyard, 33, 152
Klebold, Dylan, 143, 145

Kleck, Gary: crime and assault
weapons and, 45; gun "buybacks"
and, 37; right-to-carry laws and, 78;
"Saturday night specials" and, 50;
self-defense and, 9
Klein, M. Christine, 139
Kmart, 142
Kopel, David, 156
Korda, Michael, 115, 143
Ku Klux Klan, 51

LaPierre, Wayne, ix, 21, 54
Late Night with Conan O'Brien, 140
Lautenberg, Frank, 29, 30
Law Enforcement Alliance of America,
77
Lawrence Research, 171
Lee, Spike, 143
Left, 140, 151
Letterman, David, 141
Levi Strauss, 128
Levy, Chandra, 70
Levy, Robert, 113
Lexington, Mass., 117, 119
Liberia, 150
liberty. *See* freedom
Library of Congress, 35
Libya, 42
Lieberman, Joseph, 13, 14, 28; AGS
and, 126; background checks and,
30–31; gun shows and, 84
Lindgren, James, 117
litigation, gun control and, 131–37
Livy, 107
Lopez, Jennifer, 107
Los Angeles Times, 119
Lott, John R., Jr., 63, 74; antigun
groups and, 122–23; child accidents
and, 97; gun control and crime and,
7–8; right-to-carry laws and, 77–78;
women and gun ownership and, 80
Louisiana, 65, 136
Luby's cafeteria, 59–60, 76, 173
Lumpe, Lora, 150

MacArthur Foundation, 127, 134
Mackenzie, Frederick, 117
Madison, James, 3, 107, 187
Magaw, John, 90
Magna Carta, 108, 152
Maine, 65
Mali, 159
Mao Tse-tung, 129

Marcus Aurelius, 107
Maryland, 39–40; ballistic fingerprinting and, 48; gun availability and, 67–68; gun control and, 71–72; gun ownership in, 65–66
Mason, George, 50, 105
McCain, John: AGS and, 14, 126; background checks and, 30–31; campaign finance reform and, 13–15, 23, 133; gun safety and, 14; gun shows and, 25–26, 28–29, 84
McDonald's, 180
McGuire, Phillip, 42
McKelvey, Andrew, 169; AGS and, 14–15, 126
media: "assault weapons" and, 45; campaign finance reform and, 13; freedom and, 184; gun availability and, 62–63; gun control and, 7, 17, 21–24; Million Mom March and, 140–41; opposition to gun ownership and, 19; plastic gun sham and, 42; self-defense stories and, 7–8; sensationalism and, 22; victims of crimes and, 3
Media Research Center, 22
Meese, Ed, 85
Meet the Press, 54
Miami, Fla., 134
Miami Herald, 86
Michigan, 11, 24, 162
Middle East, 25–26
"Military Sniper Weapon Regulation Act," 49
Miller, Greg, 88
Miller, Zell, 162, 170; "Picket Line of Freedom" of, 183–89
Million Mom March, 66, 124, 140–41
Milwaukee, Wisc., 165
Mineta, Norman, 90
Minutemen, 114, 119
Missouri, 123–24
Mobile, Ala., 56
Monster.com, 14
Montana, 65
Moore, Michael, 81
More, Sir Thomas, 128
More Guns, Less Crime (Lott), 74
Morgan, Edmund, 114
Morial, Marc, 136
Mormon Church, 116
Mothers Against Drunk Driving, 150
Movieline magazine, 141

movies, guns in, 143–47
Mustard, David B., 77–78

National Association of Chiefs of Police, 135
National Center for Health Statistics, 40, 95
National Center for Injury Prevention and Control, 40
National Center for Policy Analysis, 31, 136
National Endowment for the Humanities (NEH), 118
National Firearms Act (1934), 52, 112
national ID cards, 58, 91–92, 129
National Instant Check System (NICS): gun shows and, 27, 30–31; Justice Department and, 11; law enforcement and, 56–57
National Institute of Justice, 7, 27, 98
National Institute on Mental Health, 147
National Journal, 131
National Review Online, 115
National Rifle Association (NRA): background checks and, 30; ballistic fingerprinting and, 48; campaign finance reform and, 13–14; "cop-killer" bullets hoax and, 36; Democratic Party and, 162–63, 166, 183; gun locks and, 38, 40; gun safety and, 14; gun safety education and, 16, 94–96, 99; gun-safety legislation and, 17; hunting and, 102–3; Institute for Legislative Action of, 11; litigation and, 136–37; as NGO, 150; plastic guns and, 43; police and, 73; sport shooting and, 180–81; women and, 16
National Safety Council, 40, 95
National Sheriffs' Association, 95
National Sporting Goods Association, 179
National Zoo shooting, 38, 66–68
Natural Born Killers, 143, 145
natural law, 107
NBC, 21–22, 44, 54, 165
Nebraska, 6
NEH. *See* National Endowment for the Humanities
New England Journal of Medicine, 125
New Jersey, 72
Newkirk, Ingrid, 100

New Mexico, 133
New Orleans, La., 133, 134, 135
Newsweek, 167
New York, 72, 133
New York Post, 133
New York Review of Books, 114
New York Times, 81, 117, 135, 159, 186
New York Times Book Review, 114
NGOs. *See* nongovernmental organi-
    zations
NICS. *See* National Instant Check
    System
nongovernmental organizations
    (NGOs), 22–23; antigun group
    funding and, 127–28; international
    gun control and, 150
Noonan, Peggy, 163
North Korea, 149
North Valley Jewish Community Cen-
    ter, 46
Northwestern University, 62, 117
Norton, Eleanor Holmes, 67
Norwegian Initiative on Small Arms
    Transfers, 150
NRA. *See* National Rifle Association
Nugent, Ted, 98–99

O'Donnell, Rosie, 21, 139, 141, 142,
    169
Oak Park, Ill., 71
Odighizuwa, Peter, 7–8
Oklahoma, 143
Olson, Theodore, 105–6, 113
Olson, Walter, 132, 135
Oregon, 16, 78, 169
Orwell, George, 69
Ovid, 107

Pacelle, Wayne, 100
Paine, Thomas, 187
Panic Room, 144
The Patriot, 144
PBS, 118
Pence, Shawnra, 79
Peninsula Daily News, 79
Penn, Schoen & Berland, 15
People for the Ethical Treatment of
    Animals (PETA), 100, 129
Perdicaris, Ion, 83
PETA. *See* People for the Ethical
    Treatment of Animals
Philadelphia, Pa., 133, 136, 165
Philippines, 150
Phoenix, Ariz., 87

Physicians for Social Responsibility,
    125, 151
pilots, arming of, 89–91
Pitofsky, Robert, 146
plastic gun sham, 18, 41–43
Plato, 107
police: gun control and, 72–74; killing
    of, 46; law enforcement and, 5;
    NRA and, 73; response time of,
    64–65; self-defense and, 63–65; vic-
    tims of crimes and, 3
Police Athletic League, 95
politicians: "assault weapons" and, 45;
    gun ownership and, 69; opposition
    to gun ownership and, 19
Pol Pot, 129
Polsby, Daniel D., 37
The Practice, 131
Prevention of Crime and the Treat-
    ment of Offenders, 156
Price, John and Carole, 93–94
Project CUFF (Criminal Use of
    Firearms by Felons), 56
Project Exile, 54–55, 56, 74
Project Safe Neighborhoods, 56
"Protection of Lawful Commerce in
    Arms Act," 183–84
Public Citizen, 128

al-Qaddafi, Muammar, 42

Rainmaker, 131
Rand, Kristen, 90
Rauch, Jonathan, 131
Reagan, Ronald, 10, 43, 111
Reed, Jack, 29
registration: ballistic fingerprinting
    and, 47–48; confiscation and,
    31–34, 43, 70–71
Relman, Arnold S., 125
Rendell, Ed, 133–34
Reno, Janet, 54, 56
Republican Party, 162
responsibility, gun ownership and, ix,
    57, 96
Rhode Island, 6
Richards, Ann, 77
Richmond, Va., 54, 61, 74
Richmond Times-Dispatch, 8
RICO, 85–86
right-to-carry laws: in America, 74–75;
    in Florida, 64–65; Second Amend-
    ment and, 6; "shall issue," 5, 75;
    success of, 74–78

right to keep and bear arms: Constitution and, 3; freedom and, 57; history of, 108–9; Second Amendment and, ix, 2, 59
Rivera, Geraldo, 142
robbery: in America, 5; property and, 3
Roberts, Will Craig, 49
Rock, Allan, 32
Roosevelt, Franklin, 88, 111, 162
Roosevelt, Theodore, 44, 83, 99, 102
Rosenthal, Steve, 167
Rowan, Carl, 69–70
Russert, Tim, 54
Russia. *See* Soviet Union
Ryker, James, 78–79

Safer, Morley, 125
safety locks. *See* gun locks
St. Louis, Mo., 165
Salt Lake City, Utah, 73
The Samurai, the Mountie, and the Cowboy (Kopel), 156
San Francisco International Airport, 88
Sara Lee, 14, 128
"Saturday night specials," 23, 49–52
Schumer, Chuck, 11, 25, 35, 56; gun shows and, 84
Science, 147
Scotland, 33
Scott, James Edward, 63
Seckora, Melissa, 115, 117–18
Second Amendment: in action, 118–19; African-Americans and, 51; civil rights and, 52; crime and, 18, 59–60; crime rates and, 18; defense of, 14; Founders and, 2, 57–58, 106, 108–9, 111; freedom and, 2, 129; Great Britain and, 119–20; meaning of, 18, 105–20; natural law and, 107; protection of, ix; public security and, 2; purpose of, 59; rights of, 5; right-to-carry laws and, 6; right to keep and bear arms and, ix, 2, 59; self-defense and, 59, 107–9; terrorism and, 18, 82, 92
self-defense: in America, 119; crime and, 7; Founders and, 108; gun control and, 33, 59–80; guns and, 7–10; police and, 63–65; rights and, 65; "Saturday night specials" and, 49; Second Amendment and, 59, 107–9
Selleck, Tom, 142
semi-automatic firearms: "assault weapons" and, 7, 21–22; automatic

firearms and, 44; cosmetic attachments for, 7; crime and, 45; criminals and, 45. *See also* "assault weapons"
Senate Judiciary Committee, 54
September 11 attacks, 10, 11, 81, 84
Sequim, Wash., 79
Serafin, Barry, 122–23
Sessions, Jeff, 36, 56
Shakespeare, William, 144
"shall issue" right-to-carry laws, 5, 75
Shamall, Mohammed Tawfiq, 86
Sheen, Martin, 139–40, 165
Sherrill, Robert, 51
Shoney's restaurant, 60–61
Sierra Club, 150
silencers, 53
Simon & Schuster, 115
60 Minutes, 43, 125
Skokie, Ill., 62
Sky Harbor International Airport, 87
"smart guns," 97–98
Smith, Ben, 62
Snyder, Jeffrey R., 174; advice given to victims and, 3; crime and morality and, 3–5; self-defense and, 79
"soccer moms." *See* women
Soros, George, 127, 134
South Africa, 150
South Dakota, 136
Soviet Union, 10, 128–29, 150
sport shooting: benefits of, 179–80; gun safety and, 98–99; popularity of, 179; Second Amendment and, 59
Springfield, Ore., 78
Sprint, 128
Statute of Winchester of 1285, 108
Stone, Oliver, 143
Stone, Sharon, 141
Strickland, Tom, 168–69
Sugarmann, Josh, 44
suicide, 7, 152
Sweden, 152
Switzerland, 151
Syracuse University, 55

Taiwan, 158
Tennessee, 51, 165
The Ten Things You Can't Say in America (Elder), 141
terrorism: airport security and, 87–89; America and, 5; arming pilots and, 89–91; background checks and, 81; border control and, 91–92;

terrorism *(continued)*
  crime and, 18; foreign policy and, 83–84; freedom and, 84–86; gun control and, 1–19, 10–13, 81–82, 86–87; gun shows and, 14, 18, 24–31, 84–85; in Middle East, 25–26; Second Amendment and, 18, 82, 92
Terry, Thomas, 60–61
Texas, 24, 26, 59–60, 76–77, 140
Texas Exile, 77
Thomases, Susan, 141
Thurston High School, 78
Time Warner, 128, 144
Today show, 22
Tokyo Bar Association, 155
Toledo, Ohio, 165
Townsend, Kathleen Kennedy, 39
TRAC. *See* Transactional Records Access Clearinghouse
Transactional Records Access Clearinghouse (TRAC), 55
Transportation Department, 90–91
Transportation Security Administration, 90
Treasury Department, 36; "Saturday night specials" and, 49
trigger locks. *See* gun locks
Tueller, Dennis, 73
Tulsa, Okla., 49
Turner, Jim, 167

UN. *See* United Nations
Unified Sportsmen of Florida, 75
United Flight 93, 1, 2, 173
United Nations (UN), international gun control and, 18, 149, 156–59
United States. *See* America
United States Conference of Mayors, 128
University of California at Berkeley, 15
Unsafe Handgun Act, 135
U.S. Bureau of Justice Statistics, 27
U.S. Consumer Product Safety Commission, 39
U.S. News & World Report, 101
U.S. v. Miller, 111–13
USA Today, 122, 163
"Use NICS in Terrorism Investigations Act," 11
USS *Cole*, 84
Utopia, gun control and, 128–29

vandalism, 5
Vanity Fair, 39
Very Rich Individuals (VRIs), antigun group funding and, 126–27
Viacom, 13
Vietnam, 117, 159
Vincent, Billie, 42
Violence Policy Center, 44; agenda of, 124–25; antique guns and, 49; arming pilots and, 90; funding for, 127; gun safety education and, 96; self-defense and, 65; terrorism and gun control and, 10
Virginia, 7–8, 54, 67–68
Vogue, 100

waiting periods: Brady Act and, 6; crime and, 35; danger of, 18, 34–35; gun control and, 13
Wal-Mart, 180
Washburn, Patrick S., 121–22
Washington (state), 79
Washington, D.C.: gun availability and, 66–70; gun control and, 72; homicide in, 37, 45; National Zoo shooting in, 38, 66–68; law enforcement and, 61
Washingtonian, 100
Washington Post, 8, 47, 100
Washington Times, 36, 158
Watts, J. C., 143
Wayans, Keenen Ivory, 145
Wayne State College, 118
Wellstone, Paul, 13–14, 15
West Palm Beach, Fla., 165
West Wing, 139–40, 165
Wheeler, Tim, 125
White, Glen, 77
Will, George F., 64–65
Williams, Anthony, 67
Williams, Pete, 21–22
Wills, Garry, 114
Wirthlin, Richard, 2
women: AGS and, 16; gun ownership and, 5, 16, 79–80; NRA and, 16; "Saturday night specials" and, 52
Wyoming, 65

Young, Cathy, 151
Young, Don, 102
YWCA, 128

Zigler, Ken, 72–74